All the best –

Chris Coleman.

The Green Banana Papers
Marketing Secrets for Technology Entrepreneurs

Chris Coleman

St.
Barthélemy
press.

S
P

St. Barthélemy Press
Atlanta, GA 30341
www.saintbartsbooks.com

The Green Banana Papers: Marketing Secrets for Technology Entrepreneurs
Copyright © 2001 by Chris Coleman

Printed in Canada

Creative direction: Dan Hansen
Design and typography: Mary Erna Scovel
Graphic production: Jenny Sercer
Cover photograph: Jerry Siegel

ISBN: 1-887617-02-7

This book is dedicated to
David Dunn-Rankin

And to
John Coleman
Alexandra Arnold
Bridgitt Arnold
Caroline Amory
Mary Yaeger
Norm Yaeger
Frank O. Smith
And all the wonderful people at Folio Z

Acknowledgements

First and foremost, my thanks to everyone at Folio Z who spurred me on as I wrote this book. You can't imagine how important your encouragement has been. My deepest appreciation to Caroline Amory, Alexandra Arnold, Sheree Boger, Tammi Buffington, Sandy Cash, Myra Collum, Angie Cook, Laurina Florio, Carolyn Grant, Dan Hansen, Kia Holland, Paul Johnson, Yetunde Jude, Cara Koshlap, Terry McLane, Philip Mowris, Katie Paulk, Wilma Simons, Mary Erna Scovel, Jenny Sercer, Geoff Tarr, Joe Turner, Moira Vetter (and her invaluable writer's inspiration kit), Jock Whitehouse, Stefanie Weinstein, Mike Landman of 3rd Wave, Shannon Kinnard of Idea Station, and André Dawkins of Body Logic, who knows it's the last rep that counts.

My sincere appreciation to Randy Smith at By Design, Clarke Bishop at TutorMe.com, Ricky Steele at PricewaterhouseCoopers, Tripp Rackley at Digital Insight, Mark Firmin, Tom Clements, Michael Reene at 3MC, George McConnell, Bob Lasher at Application Partners, Craig Miller at MA&A, Rusty Gordon at iFleet, Don Schrenk and Bernard Westwood at Multisoft, Charlie Paparelli at Paparelli Ventures, David Simmons at The Technology Association of Georgia, Alf Nucifora of The Nucifora Consulting Group, and all you guys who asked for anonymity (you know who you are)!

This book wouldn't exist without a New Year's resolution to the Good Old Girls—Luba Brock, Emma Morris, and Barbara Stafford—or gentle prodding from Marilynn Mobley of Acorn Consulting Group and Walt Fuller of St. Barthélemy Press.

Finally, love and heartfelt thanks again to John Coleman, Mooey, and Loo Loo.

Good marketers have enough patience to buy green bananas.

CONTENTS

PREFACE

Over the past 14 years I've seen millions of dollars spent, misspent, and overspent by technology marketers. And I've noticed predictable patterns in the way tech companies launch, brand, and promote themselves.

On the whole, they make similar mistakes, reach similar conclusions, and make similar decisions at predictable stages in their firm's life.

If you're a technology entrepreneur—or a marketing professional working for one—you'll probably do the same thing. But forewarned is forearmed, and it's helpful to know in advance what works and what doesn't.

This book is based on firsthand experience helping hundreds of clients market technology products and services. Some have participated in the Folio Z Green Banana™ program and messaging workshops; others have been retainer clients or project-by-project accounts. No matter what the relationship, I've learned something priceless from every one of them. It is their collective wisdom you'll find in these pages.

Help yourself to anything that makes sense. But remember, in the long run you'll do exactly what feels right at the time. And don't worry about it. For better or for worse, that's how marketing works.

INTRODUCTION

This isn't a textbook about marketing theory. It's a book for entrepreneurs who want to know how marketing works in real life. It's for people who want straightforward advice about how to spend their money more wisely—and how to quit feeling like they're being taken when they plunk down $10,000 for a quarter-page ad. It's for executives who want to communicate better with their marketing staff, and for anybody who wouldn't mind being the kind of client that agencies jump through hoops for.

Plenty has already been written on how to write a marketing plan, develop a marketing budget, and determine lead-to-sale ratios on direct mail campaigns. If that's what you're looking for, check the resources at the end of this book. On these pages are an inside look at the mindsets and assumptions that can cause your marketing to succeed or fail.

There's no need to read this book sequentially or cover-to-cover. It's a compilation of observations that have been gathered over time, jotted down on thousands of pieces of scrap paper, and finally collected into a book. Each section makes sense on its own, so start and stop anywhere you like.

A final word: you won't agree with everything on these pages. Marketing is a dialogue, after all, and interesting dialogues have their share of conflicting ideas. What matters is that you come away with a heartfelt commitment to telling your company's story clearly, consistently, and convincingly. That's the most powerful marketing tool in the world.

Another Way To Think About Marketing

- *Simplify your life: forget the four Ps*
- *The marketer's cheatsheet*

SIMPLIFY YOUR LIFE:
FORGET THE FOUR PS

Developers at the first software company I worked for used to call the eighth floor, where the advertising people worked, "the black hole of profits." I didn't think it was funny then, but over the years I've come to understand their point of view.

For an entrepreneur, especially one with an engineering or finance background, it's unnerving to watch the marketing department soak up money with no guarantee there will be a quick payback—or any payback at all. I've worked with thousands of IT executives, and they all have the same complaint about marketing: they can't measure the results.

The real issue is more basic. They don't know what marketing is, so they don't know what to measure. And the problem is made worse by marketing people who are just as confused as their clients/bosses are. They're just better at covering it up.

Who can blame them? It's hard to grasp a discipline defined by its own trade group, the American Marketing Association, as "the process of planning and executing the conception, pricing, promotion, and distribution of ideas, goods, and services to create exchanges that satisfy individual and organizational objectives."

Forget that. This is the real world, where the four Ps—product, position, promotion, place—make their first and last group appearance in your formal marketing plan. They are important strategically, but they're too ambiguous for anybody in your company to relate to day-to-day.

Hammer home one simple mantra: *Marketing is everything you do to influence a positive buying decision—both now and a hundred years from now.* The beauty of this description is simplicity and scope. It's big enough to encompass lifelong initiatives like branding, and it's specific enough to remind us why we're in business at all: to make a sale.

Marketing is a process, not an event. It's a long-term proposition, not a pre-IPO tactic. It demands patience, persistence, and steady trudging. It has nothing to do with glamour and everything to do with perseverance.

Why technology CEOs hate the "M" word

I've often wondered why otherwise even-keeled CEOs take their company's marketing mistakes personally, and I've decided there are four reasons.

First, they secretly think if they were *really* good at their jobs the mistake never would have happened. Entrepreneurs don't like to fail at anything, and they definitely don't like to think of themselves as half-baked marketers.

Second, they don't know who to trust now that so-and-so's let them down. On average, 50% of entrepreneurs sever their first ad agency relationship within 12 to 15 months. The break is often triggered by mistakes that more seasoned firms take in stride.

Third, marketing missteps are usually made in public. Enough said.

Fourth, they can't stand to see all that money go down the drain.

If it's any consolation, there is no successful technology company on the planet that *hasn't* made serious marketing blunders, usually over and over again.

Don't let the jargon fool you

You're not the only company founder who's fuzzy—all right,

clueless—about audience segmentation and target response rates. Your job is to figure out who *does* know what they're talking about and develop a working relationship with them.

This business is replete with jargon. It's easy to get trapped in a conversation larded with phrases like "let's focus on strategic one-to-one marketing to maximize the buyer experience and increase our value-add."

Dig out your shovel and find out if there's anything underneath before you commit to working with anybody who talks like this, and don't discount your own business sense when making this assessment. As Al Ries puts it, "What's a management person, anyway? A marketing person who can read a balance sheet and a profit-and-loss statement."

Good ad agencies with strong IT experience—and there are many of them—will respond in plain English, not jargon, when you ask what they can do for you. They won't flinch when you broach touchy subjects like account executives who don't understand your business and sales leads that don't pan out. Most important, they won't pretend to know something they don't.

Once you find good marketing talent—both on staff and at an agency—your job is to be a good client. It's no fun to work for someone who doesn't understand or appreciate what they're paying for. From your perspective, becoming a knowledgeable buyer is the best way to get your money's worth.

What marketing won't do, no matter how much money you've got:

It won't overcome a bad product or lousy service.

It won't close the deal.

It won't compensate for an incompetent sales force or poor distribution.

It won't work overnight.

So what will marketing do?

It will make your company visible, credible, and memorable.

And until that happens, nothing happens.

THE MARKETER'S CHEATSHEET

The marketing terms people fling around every day are clear as mud, but nobody wants to come right out and say, "What in the world does positioning *mean*, anyway?" Here's a quick reference.

Strategy At a Glance

Branding
- Culture and values based
- Makes a promise
- Consistent and predictable
- Builds long-term corporate value

Marketing
- Product and buyer based
- Offers a solution
- Builds market share

Positioning
- The context in which buyers view you
- Supports your USP (unique selling proposition)
- Goal is to build market dominance

Targeting
- Find the buyer whose hair's on fire
- Tweak your product just for him
- Goal is to build references

Tactics at a Glance

Advertising
- One-to-many: "Hey, you!"
- Creates perceived value for product/company
- Supports the brand
- Subjective, long-term payback
- Impact is cumulative

Direct Marketing
- One-to-one: "Hey, Mike!"
- Creates a "buy now" situation
- Supports sales goals
- Focused and urgent
- Quick, quantifiable payback
- Impact is immediate

Sales Promotion
- Induces trial of the product
- Focused and short-term
- Product and price-based
- Goal: build volume at competitors' expense

Public Relations
- Creates third-party credibility
- Solidifies the brand
- Focused and long-term
- Message-based
- Goals: credibility, damage control

2

YOUR PRODUCT: WHAT ARE YOU REALLY SELLING?

- *Guess what? You're the brand*

- *Seven questions to ask before you go to market*

- *"Our biggest competitor's Microsoft."* Yeah, right

- *Fear of focus*

- *Positioning: there's no perfect answer, so don't waste time looking for it*

GUESS WHAT?
YOU'RE THE BRAND

"We've got a terrific brand. We just have to make the market aware of it," the VP of marketing at a 12-month-old Internet company told me recently. "What can your agency do for us?"

The first thing my agency can do is point out (politely) that he doesn't have a brand. He has a product. Brands are built of blood, sweat, and tears, and they take a lot longer than 12 months to develop. In fact, purists argue that no company less than five years

14   old can claim an established brand.

Brands are an outgrowth of what companies are, not what they do. Simply put, your brand is your firm's *personality and promise to your customer*.

Until you've expressed that personality and fulfilled that promise so often, and so consistently, that your customers can articulate in their own words what you stand for, you don't have a brand.

You can't calculate or contrive a brand, and you can't test a few prototypes to see which one plays best in the market. It's simpler than that. Just take a good, hard look at your own values, beliefs, and motivations. As an entrepreneur, your company is a direct reflection of your personality and character. Customers are buying *you* and what *you* represent. You are the brand.

Walt Disney, Elvis Presley, Tom Shane ("your friend in the diamond business"), and Jane Fonda are entrepreneurs whose enterprises were built on the strength of a personal brand. Whether you buy their products or agree with their philosophies is irrelevant. *No brand on the planet is beloved by all.*

"I think one of the biggest misconceptions is that our brand was carefully designed, carefully executed, carefully thought out from day one," Martha Stewart once told a reporter. "It was not. It was the fortuitous result of extremely hard work."

By acting consistently on a fundamental belief—that a gracious lifestyle is within anyone's reach, not just the privileged—Stewart built a billion-dollar company and a priceless brand.

The concept of CEO as brand is more than a theory. *Marketing Computers* polled 4,500 IT professionals in 1999 to determine the brand perceptions of technology leaders. The survey data, along with an analysis of each firm's stock performance and media coverage, were used to rank chief executives with the best brand reputations in the industry.

At the top of the list is Michael Dell ("he is Dell's trusted brand"), followed by Bill Gates ("household name, but image in downslide"), Steve Jobs ("the ultimate communicator"), Steve Case ("young, but steady builder of AOL's power-brand"), and Scott McNealy ("consistent leadership; embodies the brand"). These people have built franchises that extend beyond products, distribution, and patents. The sustaining power of their brands is in their personal attributes as leaders.

If you are uncomfortable in the limelight, this will be one of your greatest hurdles as a CEO. Quite simply, your company's growth depends upon how well you handle your public role.

This issue is very difficult for entrepreneurs who don't distinguish between self-promotion and narcissism. They are convinced that if they do excellent work and satisfy their customers, the rest will happen naturally.

That's a good start, but it's not enough if you want to grow something bigger than a 20- or 30-person organization. As the embodiment of your firm's brand, you *must* be visible, articulate, and constantly creating opportunities to tell your story.

As CEO, your job is to develop recognition in ever-widening circles beyond your company. Unless the people who

16   influence your success—media, competitors, potential employees, analysts—know who *you* are and what you stand for, the biggest marketing budget in the world can't build an enduring brand.

Seven Questions To Ask Before You Go To Market

A few tech companies still think "marketable product" is redundant. "Hey, the product exists, doesn't it? Of course it's marketable. Just find me a buyer smart enough to appreciate it."

It doesn't work that way. Products fail for one of four reasons: the deliverable is incomplete, it's just too complicated to use, the positioning is off, or it's a me-too offering.

(This assumes the launch was adequately funded and the marketing was sustained enough to be effective.)

It's incomplete. Geoff Moore, author of *Crossing the Chasm* and other classics, articulated the concept of "the whole product" nearly ten years ago, and it's as valid today as it was then. The whole product is a complete solution—everything the customer needs, besides your product, to make a compelling reason to buy.

This means your development strategy must take into account the distribution channels, training, on-site engineering, post-sale support, and hardware or software necessary to make your product perform perfectly.

This is a stumbling block for international IT firms launching in the U.S. Being the big dog in Europe or Australia, where the territory is smaller and the referral network tighter, doesn't prepare them for the sprawling discontinuity of U.S. markets. Alliances take much longer to form and referenceable accounts take longer to develop. The more portable and self-sufficient your product, the faster you'll see a return.

It's too complicated. Solutions too complex to move smoothly through the channel are doomed to failure. Products that disrupt the end user's existing processes, no matter how inefficient those processes are, have less than a 50/50 chance of survival. And "sandwich" products—those that rely completely on another manufacturer's front-end and back-end systems—are among the toughest of all to sell.

It's improperly positioned. Assess the competitive landscape and the buyer's current alternatives *before* you fall in love with developing The Next Big Thing. Some marketers believe there's one, and only one, position for any product, but I'm not among them. Don't spend a year analyzing spreadsheets and competitive reports to pick the perfect place on the map. Your sweet spot (particularly for business-to-business products) is always bigger than a pinhead, and there's room to move around within reason.

The only thing worse than a "cowboy" engineer who designs what the market doesn't want is a "cowboy" sales rep, who promises to reengineer the product to get the sale.

—*25-year marketing veteran at an analytical instrumentation company*

It's a me-too idea. Some people don't realize they've built a me-too product until they look for a PR firm to represent them. Good agencies won't accept an account they can't promote.

Dr. Mark Goulston, a Santa Monica-based marketing consultant, tells his clients to ask themselves seven questions before they write a single line of code. Here's his list. Feel free to post in your R&D department.

Question #1: What can you do for me?

People don't care what you can do until they know what you

can *get done* for them. Products or services whose benefits require "too much brain space, focus, and follow-through" to use simply won't fly.

Question #2: Why is that important to me?

Customers are looking for something *they* want to buy, not something you want to sell them. "If all they care about in a PDA is storing data, backing it up easily and fitting the thing into their shirt pocket, then they'll choose a Palm Pilot over a Psion," says Goulston.

Question #3: Is it more than I'm getting now?

Whether people own up to it or not, everybody wants more. If you're not offering more—significantly more, in fact, than the status quo—rethink the product or shelve the idea.

Question #4: Is it better than I'm getting now?

Answering "yes" to the previous question isn't enough. Quantity won't compensate for poor quality.

Question #5: Is it sooner than I'm getting it now?

Time is money. Save the buyer lots of time and you've got the potential to make lots of money.

Question #6: Does it cost less than I'm spending now?

This applies to both business-to-business and consumer markets.

Question #7: Is it less risky than what I'm doing now?

Perceived risk goes up in direct proportion to the price and number of decision-makers involved.

Understanding what buyers experience before, during, and after using their product separates successful companies from the duds. The best way to do this is to have your development staff and your marketing people meet prospective customers face-to-face—in person, not behind a one-way mirror in the usability lab.

"OUR BIGGEST COMPETITOR'S MICROSOFT." YEAH, RIGHT

In the survey we send to participants prior to the Folio Z messaging workshop, we ask, among other things, "Who are your competitors?" Somebody always mentions Microsoft.

This is either wishful thinking or a gross misunderstanding of the definition of "competitor." A 200-person Internet company is not competing with Microsoft.

When analyzing your competition, don't

get carried away with all the choices your prospects can make: in-house, no decision, Microsoft, the Chinese Embassy. In reality, you're up against two to five companies roughly your same size. As you move up or down in your niche, or change niches completely, those competitors change.

Don't waste time figuring out how to compete in a market already dominated by a company with more than 25% share. Go vertical, go regional, or tailor your offering for an underserved segment of a larger market.

Why? Because any company with a 25% share owns that market. When it does slip, it's picked off by the number-two player. Your goal is to be first or second in every sector you occupy. If you can't realistically gain that position through an aggressive acquisition strategy, look for another niche. Clawing your way up from third or fourth place through organic growth is virtually impossible.

Objectivity is important when assessing your competition. Entrepreneurs hate losing deals to anybody they think is below them on the food chain, so they tend to discount up-and-coming players.

Don't rule anybody out without getting another opinion. It's a blow to the ego to think your prospects might take a new player seriously, especially when you've enjoyed the lead position for awhile. But it's a mistake to ignore any competitor, and you certainly won't see them coming if you're focused on Microsoft.

Who's your competition?

The brand leader? This one's tough to unseat in an established category. Think twice.

The number-two player? Prepare to compete on price, availability or service.

Nobody? Welcome to "create your own category" country. And you'd better get the analysts on your side.

Entrepreneurs and salespeople don't look at the competitive landscape the same way. Entrepreneurs underestimate their competitors and salespeople see every Tom, Dick, and Harry as a threat. This is why research is important. Making decisions without an objective view of the market is like drinking your own bathwater.

Ongoing third-party phone surveys are one of the best ways to stay in touch with your market, and an outbound telemarketing/teleresearch program is a good investment.

Choose a vendor experienced in the technology industry. (This is vital.) The goal is to contact everyone in your client and prospect database at least once, and preferably more often, over the course of a year.

26   *Research is not for the gutless*

It takes courage to ask for feedback. You won't always like what you hear. Don't shoot the messenger, don't quit asking the tough questions, and don't ignore or discount criticism.

When can you declare victory?

You dominate your target segment when:

- *Objective third parties refer to you as the leader*

- *You begin to get unsolicited leads from target prospects*

- *Other vendors in the segment tout that they are compatible with your product*

- *Hard-to-reach people routinely return your phone calls*

                    —*Geoffrey Moore Consulting*

A year or so ago, I got a call from an irate client who was offended by research indicating his firm was virtually unknown in the United States. He couldn't believe the company's German track record carried no weight with American buyers.

"We're number one in the world!" he said. "We've got 138

installations, and our closest competitor has less than 50!" Although all 50 of the competitor's installations were blue-chip, referenceable, and U.S.-based, he felt this was irrelevant.

We had recommended limiting the U.S. launch to one vertical segment with pent-up demand and good expansion potential. Senior management in Germany turned the idea down flat, saying the approach was demeaning for a market leader.

The client went on about the useless data, then threw in a parting jab before hanging up. "Just to give you an idea of how bad this research is," he yelled, "not *one person* in this company has read it!"

F E A R   O F   F O C U S

Unless you have bottomless pockets and unlimited time, you must choose a market segment and stay there until you own it. It's impossible to market horizontally and win.

There are no exceptions to this rule. None. It's as inevitable as death and taxes, but entrepreneurs fight it every day. Every time a prospective client tells me, "this is a truly horizontal application…anybody can use it," I know there's a hard road ahead.

Focus entails sacrifice, which is why it's

such a difficult decision. Who wants to limit themselves to one opportunity when the table's laden with so many? Besides, what if we make the wrong choice?

There is no perfect target market, so don't waste time looking for it. But there are usually two or three good options, and that's plenty to choose from. Look for these characteristics.

Don't confuse the term "market segment" with "vertical focus." Although vertical focus can be an attribute of a segment, market segments can also be defined in terms of technology, customer size, geography, or type of solution.

—Jerry Nulton, KeyLink Systems

You know and understand the buyers. You've been in their shoes—or pretty close to it—and you can identify a decision-maker with the authority to spend money on your product or service. If you can't identify one person (by name, title, or function) with *both* these qualifications (makes decisions and approves expenditures) your offering isn't defined clearly enough.

Their hair's on fire. Something bad is happening, and you can fix it right now. This buyer's got a real problem and knows it. Equally important, he or she is motivated to do something about it. Inertia is your number-one competitor, so don't fight it if you can't win.

Your differentiator is obvious, it matters to the buyer, and it's available now. Is your product or service completely ready to ship/install/use? If not, when will it be? Selling futures is dangerous business. The buyer's hair is on fire, remember? He/she won't forgive *or* forget if the product doesn't deliver on time or work as promised.

Advice from the field

"Don't try to be everything to everyone."

> —*Randy Smith,*
> *CEO, By Design, Inc.*

"Define your market."

> —*Michael Reene,*
> *CEO, 3rd Millennium Communications, Inc.*

"Find a niche, build a reputation, and stick to your knitting."

> —*Robert Lasher,*
> *President, Application Partners, Inc.*

There's room to grow. You want the competition to be weak, scattered, or nonexistent. Segments with a clear leader, a clear challenger, and a wannabe or two in the mix are a bad bet. Forget them, no matter how lucrative they look. You can't unseat a market leader with a conventional "faster, better, cheaper" strategy, and dominance is what you're after.

32   Find a segment where you can claim a 20% to 25% share and move to adjacent sectors as you grow. Simply put, go where your differentiator will truly be appreciated and there's enough business to sustain your company over the long haul.

POSITIONING: THERE'S NO PERFECT ANSWER, SO DON'T WASTE TIME LOOKING FOR IT

Choosing your target market, and your position within it, isn't a matter of life and death. One of the toughest ideas for technology entrepreneurs to grasp is the value—no, the necessity—of going to market with a less-than-watertight strategy.

There are at least two viable launch points for your offering, perhaps more. Give up the notion that the "right" answer is out there, and when you find it the skies will open and rays of sunlight will light your path.

You've heard this before, but it's worth repeating: *perfectionists don't win in high-growth industries.* Winners get that way through initiative, unflagging focus on the buyer, and acting quickly even when they don't have all the answers.

This was brought home to me recently when a client we'd been serving for over a year missed a critical market opportunity. The product was extremely promising and the competitive landscape was wide open. We conducted research, wrote a marketing plan, developed a lead-generation program and walked out of meetings all pumped up, telling each other, "OK, *now* we're ready to roll."

But then my phone rang. "Hold off on that ad," our client said. "I had lunch with so-and-so today and he says we're approaching the market from the wrong angle. Let's do a little more research."

The product never saw the light of day. The company was sold and our former client is back to work—on somebody else's payroll.

Almost is good enough

Indecision is death in this business. It's easy to get bogged down writing your company's positioning and elevator statements. (You'll find a technique for writing elevator statements in Chapter 4.) But the more perfectionistic you are, the longer it will take to get out of the planning stage and into making money.

Positioning is a stumbling block for entrepreneurs because it's a confusing concept. Textbook descriptions are fuzzy at best. The clearest definition I've ever heard is from Geoffrey Moore, who shared it at an Atlanta presentation years ago and immediately made life easier for every entrepreneur in the audience. This one's so complete and clear that there's no point in looking any further.

What is a position?

- It's what your buyer remembers when your name comes up
- It's what the other people in your market say behind your back

What's the purpose of positioning?

- To identify yourself to the market you're serving
- To present yourself as the market leader
- To get everyone in the market to support your position—including your competitors

In this context, your job is to figure out *who* your product appeals to most (your target), *what* it will do for them (your product benefits), and *why* it's superior to the current options (your differentiator).

36   *How to write a positioning statement*

Don't hammer out a position statement by yourself. Involve your management team and a cross-section of people from throughout the company in this exercise. Gather everybody around a table with a stack of forms that look like this:

Our Positioning Statement

We provide _____
               (your product or service category)

For _____
               (your target buyer)

So they can _____
               (your product's key benefit)

Unlike _____
               (these alternatives)

Our product _____
               (your differentiator)

Now start writing. Do the first draft without group discussion: the goal at this point is to capture individual points of view.

Compare notes. Have all read their statements out loud.

Go to round two, where everybody writes a second draft on fresh sheets of paper.

Repeat this exercise until the group agrees on a crisp, accurate statement. Expect ten to 20 rewrites to get to this point.

Don't rush this process. A good positioning statement is short and written in everyday language, and it takes hours of intense work to reach that level of simplicity. The final document must be something that *everybody* inside and outside the company understands and can repeat with confidence.

3

YOUR CUSTOMERS: THE GREEN BANANA THEORY

- *Pick your buyers while they're still green*
- *How to separate the nearly ripe from the nearly rotten*

PICK YOUR BUYERS WHILE THEY'RE STILL GREEN

If your sales force is chasing RFPs and your marketing department's focused exclusively on prospects already in the product evaluation stage, you can safely assume that at least half their efforts are wasted.

Most RFPs are nothing but busy work. Usually the favored supplier was identified long before the RFP is issued, so if you're not that supplier, you shouldn't be wasting time filling in the blanks.

To prospects in the evaluation stage, you're just another shark circling the pool. They are already biased in favor of the category leader. That's great if you dominate the market, but if you don't, you need to start generating awareness and credibility among a bigger base—your own green bananas.

The green banana principle is simple, and it's based on the 90/10 buying cycle. At any time, only ten percent of your target market is actually evaluating products for an immediate decision. The remaining 90 percent have either just purchased or are somewhere on the road to purchasing/repurchasing. Your job is to reach that 90 percent early and often so they hear about your company and your product from as many sources as possible.

The green banana principle is inspired by the 90-year-old who said to the produce clerk, "Honey, I'm so old I don't even buy green bananas anymore." Identify your best prospects long before they're ready to buy and market to them over the long haul. With patience, you'll cultivate a crop that pays off year after year.

The point is to get in front of your best prospects while your competitors are off chasing riper deals. It takes seven to nine impressions before your company name even registers with a buyer. Once that happens you must maintain consistent, frequent contact throughout the buying cycle. The earlier and more frequently you appear, the greater your competitive advantage.

Most companies take a short-term view of pipeline development. Business that won't close in 90 days doesn't get much attention from the sales force, and the marketing department's horizon for lead generation and qualification is usually six months or less.

This is excellent news for you. Call it buzz, call it branding, or call it being there every time your prospect turns around...whatever you call it, the green banana stage is where your marketing efforts have the greatest long-term impact with the least interference from your competition.

This strategy won't work for companies that can't build a six-to-12-month pipeline, or for companies whose resources won't cover anything that doesn't generate immediate revenue. The first is a vision problem; the second's a cash flow problem. But if you're too hungry to wait for the crop to ripen, you're doomed to spending your days fighting over leftovers.

How To Separate The Nearly Ripe From The Nearly Rotten

It only takes one or two bad customers to torpedo an emerging company. The hardest thing in the world for a young company to do is turn down business—but when juicy prospects turn into rotten clients, that's what you must do.

If you are marketing to prospects who don't value the same things you do, stop right now. The relationship can't work. Pursuing business simply to beef up your account list is

46   like marrying for money: you'll pay dearly for every dollar, and there's seldom a happy ending. Profits and morale drain away fast in the day-to-day grind of trying to please a client who doesn't see things the way you do.

For some companies a Fortune 500 account is poison. If technical innovation makes life worth living for your people, think twice before going after "the bigs." They move slowly, take few risks, and stick stubbornly to the middle of the road. Spend your marketing and sales dollars on prospects you'll enjoy working with—nimbler companies that really appreciate what you do best.

One of the worst mismatches I've seen was between an Internet development boutique and a big telecom company. The developers loved the process of building software, fiddled constantly with its deliverables, and resented the client's resistance to new ideas.

The client, on the other hand, had fought hard to get this supplier approved because he didn't have equivalent talent on staff. He was heading a new division, and outsourcing the technical support wasn't a popular move.

These two had a love-hate relationship for three years. It never occurred to the software company to wine and dine the client, and it never occurred to the client to pick up the phone and say anything good about the software. Their only personal interaction was when the VP had a technical problem or the developer needed a bill paid.

That this relationship lasted for three years is a testament to the quality of the work and the commitment (or desperation) on both sides. When the culture gap became too wide to cross, the telco didn't renew the contract and the developer lost 40% of its revenues overnight.

Signs of trouble usually appear early in the sales cycle. It's easy to ignore them if you need a cash infusion or think the name will look great on your client list. But warning signs are predictable. If more than one crops up, don't pursue the deal unless you're willing to accept the consequences.

Do these people really understand what you do? If you're a technical expert hired by the user side of the house, you have two jobs. The first is the one you've been hired to do; the second one—educating your clients—is the one that'll make you or break you. If they don't understand or appreciate what you're doing, they won't champion you when the going gets tough.

This takes two different mindsets and interpersonal styles. Have you got the talent on staff to handle both? If not, you'll spend precious billable time fighting political fires and clearing up communication problems. When the project goes dangerously over budget you're faced with an ugly dilemma: charge for the hand-holding or eat it?

Will you be cleaning up after somebody else? Thinking you can succeed where the last guy failed is a powerful ego boost, especially when you've solved the same problem a hundred times before. But if you're following previous suppliers, better find out why they've been replaced. If the mess was made in-house,

48   you could be walking into a chronic situation. Some problems can't be solved without seriously upsetting the status quo, and if that's the case, you'll be the scapegoat.

Is the firm's payment history worrisome? On average, receivables in all industries are paid in about 45 days. That means some are a lot younger...and some are a *whole* lot older. Big companies understand cash management very well, and many hang on to invoices for 60 days or more. *If you know this up front and can live with it, great.* But when a gorilla gobbles up your capacity and then takes his sweet time to pay for it, you're headed for a cash flow problem.

What attributes does your company value most in a client? What are you willing to live with? And what would cause you to say an unequivocal no? Go after accounts that fit your profile, and work toward the day that you can turn all the others down.

You'll learn the difference between ripe and rotten the hard way: through experience. No client is 100% perfect, so don't expect to find one. When the criteria that matter most to you are satisfied, take the good and live with the rest.

4

YOUR MESSAGE:
NO STORY, NO SALE

- *Match your message to your buyer's mindset*
- *Say it first and say it often*
- *The cocktail-party test*
- *Nobody loves a narcissist*

MATCH YOUR MESSAGE TO YOUR BUYER'S MINDSET

Marketing tactics aren't interchangeable. Advertising solves a different problem than direct mail, and PR isn't the answer when you're looking for short-term sales results. The tool you choose depends on where your prospect happens to be in the buying cycle.

Whether we're choosing laundry soap or an ERP system, human beings make purchasing decisions in four stages. Sometimes the process takes a few seconds; sometimes it takes years. The length of the cycle depends upon the product, the competitive environment, and the price point. Here's the sequence:

Step 1: Attention

Step 2: Credibility

Step 3: Value

Step 4: Decision

The role of marketing is to lead prospects from one step to the next *in sequence*, matching the message to the buyer's mindset at each step.

This is where many technology companies, particularly in the business-to-business sector, get off track. They short-circuit the first two stages of the buying process and skip directly to step three, the value proposition. They focus on messages about features, benefits, availability, and price and ignore one key fact: *nobody's listening*.

I call this the firehose fallacy: the belief that if you aim a torrent of information in the prospect's general direction, somebody's bound to swallow something. But the typical business manager is expected to read about a million words a week, and American adults are bombarded with 3,000 commercial messages every day. In self-protection we shut out noise that we don't understand or care about.

Step 1: Attention

The best product on the planet goes nowhere until a buyer

knows about it. Obvious? Of course. But our product is front and center of our own universe. It's easy to forget that the rest of the world doesn't know it exists.

If all your marketing focuses on a feature/benefit/value story, keep in mind that *nobody's listening yet.* Don't waste time or money on details until you have their attention.

This takes patience. I've mentioned elsewhere that your company or product name won't register on anybody's radar until they hear it seven to nine times, and that's just the beginning. Recall and recognition, the crucial first steps in brand-building, don't reach a significant level until you have repeated a single, simple message literally hundreds of times. Consistency, clarity, and frequency are the magic words.

It takes six to nine months of repeated placements to ensure that at least 60% to 70% of a publication's readership sees and reads your ad at least once.

—Merrill R. Chapman, *The Product Marketing Handbook for Software*

You will be discouraged when you don't see any sales results from your first or second or third ad. You can accelerate market awareness by increasing the frequency of your message, but this costs money. Lucent Technologies did it by spending $110 million in four months when the firm split from AT&T—but if you don't have a budget that big, be patient.

Marketing tactics useful at the first stage of the buying cycle include:

- PR
- Direct marketing (best for well-defined, compact target audiences)
- Trade shows
- Event sponsorships
- Advertising

The objective is to reach many people, many times, at the lowest cost per impression. The whole idea is to wave your arms high enough, energetically enough, and long enough to be seen above the crowd.

Step 2: Credibility

Technology buyers are notoriously unwilling to buy from a company that has no reputation, no user references, and no track record. Unless your product is an impulse item priced at two digits or less, buyers won't gamble on it until they know your reputation. Powerful product claims actually make buyers more skeptical if they've never heard of the manufacturer.

Entrepreneurs with a truly breakthrough product question this. "Look, we've developed the first so-and-so that actually works," they'll say. "Pent-up demand for this is so strong it'll practically sell itself. We don't need any corporate brochures or testimonials. People aren't buying our company—they're buying the best product on the market."

Imagine getting a call from a telemarketer offering a zero-interest home mortgage guaranteed to close in 24 hours or less, no questions asked. You *do* happen to be in the market for a new house, but you've never heard of the lender and neither has your real-estate agent. How receptive are you likely to be?

Every company sells an 11-dimension promise: delivery, specs,
options, credibility, past history, current customers, last failure,
next beta, warranty, strategic partnerships, nice lunches.

—Bill Whitman

Now imagine the call coming from Chase Manhattan Bank and referred by your real-estate agent. A good telemarketer could probably move you to the decision stage right then and there.

The best credibility builders are positive media coverage and public endorsement from customers. This, of course, is the classic chicken-or-egg dilemma. You can't get users without testimonials—and you can't get testimonials without users. There are several ways to circumvent this problem.

Ask customers to talk about why they chose your product. Tangible results are best, but when you don't have any yet, ask customers to tell why they chose your product over others. (If they had no alternative until you came along, that's even better.) Handled well, this is a powerful approach for collateral material, direct mail, your Web site, and the like. The press won't be as enthusiastic (they usually want to interview users with real results) but this is a good way to begin building your arsenal.

Produce a no-nonsense corporate brochure. When I was a copywriter, one company president actually told me, "Just make our corporate brochure look good. Nobody really reads these things—it's all marketing fluff."

People do read corporate brochures. The good ones are fast-paced, factual, and written in the first person plural ("we produce," not "they produce"). They can be as simple as a #10 trifold or as elegant as an annual report, but content is king. Don't waste money on a brochure that doesn't say anything.

Focus on PR. Positive or neutral media mentions are implicit third-party endorsements. Product reviews, executive interviews, and bylined opinion pieces are valuable and recyclable. Update your Web site every time you get a new hit. Build a clip book, keep it up to date, and put a copy in your lobby so visitors and employees always know what's happening. Order editorial reprints (call the publisher for these) and distribute them to clients, prospects, and friends of the firm.

Step 3: Value

Now that your credibility is established, the buyer's ready to hear your value proposition. In B2B markets the salesperson often steps in at this point; in the retail environment, this is where the buyer picks up your box and reads the fine print.

How many in-person calls does it take to close a sale? When 4,000 trade advertisers were asked this question, statistics showed it takes 6.60 personal sales calls to consummate a sale in the electronics and computer manufacturing industry.

—*Reed Elsevier Business Information Research, Cahners.com*

Focus on features, benefits, competitive advantages, value/price, compatibility with other products, platforms or systems, and availability. Marketing tools you'll need:

- Telesales (for lead generation and qualification)
- Product brochures
- Data sheets
- System configuration diagrams
- Cost/benefit analyses and product comparison charts
- Downloadable or trial demos

Step 4: Decision

The most vulnerable point in the sales process is the gap between the verbal OK and signing the contract. Buyer's remorse, last-ditch efforts by the competition, budget cuts, reallocations, the 11th-hour involvement of a new decision-maker—anything that *can* happen probably will. Your sales force must be able to anticipate and neutralize this possibility.

Marketing can help. A well-prepared proposal (typo-free, written in clear English, and personalized for the prospect), new customer endorsements, and a specific pricing strategy (discount for signing by a certain date, perhaps) are vital. Include a clause in the contract that grants your company permission to publish the new relationship (with the client's sign off on wording) in your marketing materials and client list.

SAY IT FIRST AND SAY IT OFTEN

Does repeating something you know you've already said drive you nuts? If so, I've got bad news.

You'll have to say it another 150 times before it sinks in.

This is the Rule of 50, and politicians understand it instinctively. The first 50 times they say something, nobody hears it. The second 50 times nobody understands it; the third 50 times nobody believes it. It's not until repetition #151 that everything clicks and people finally get it.

Entrepreneurs who think this rule doesn't apply to them are wrong. Quitting too soon is the leading cause of death for marketing ROI.

Products advertised ten times a year don't show sales increases until the fifth month of the campaign. A trade ad's effectiveness doesn't diminish until it has been run 59 times. When we're weary of our own message (or we've given up on ever being heard) the market is just beginning to pay attention.

(When you're) sick of your message, you know you're delivering it consistently enough to get across. Get to the point where you can't stand to listen to your own stump speech one more time.

—Former White House press secretary Michael McCurry,
Harvard Business Review

There's nothing about the Rule of 50 that says you have to do every repetition yourself. In fact, the goal is to make an impression on market influencers so they'll repeat your message *for* you. The effect of consistent advertising, direct mail, PR, and third-party mentions—including word-of-mouth from customers and competitors—is cumulative.

This is buzz, and it's what companies pay PR firms millions of dollars to generate.

The formula for successful marketing is simple: frequency, consistency, and clarity. It compensates for a host of short-comings, including me-too products, ho-hum advertising, and limited budgets. It's simple and foolproof, but an astonishing number of technology companies think marketing is more complicated than this.

Frequency

It takes seven to nine impressions for your company or product name to ring a bell in the mind of your prospects. Even then, they won't know who you are, what you do, or why they should care. Every impression counts at this stage, and the more the better: editorial coverage, advertising hits, employees telling people where they work, trade-show appearances, telesales calls, the greeting cards you send during the holidays...*everything*.

Once you've made a dent, you must systematically deepen and strengthen that awareness with repeated impressions. Roughly speaking (the Rule of 50 aside), the market needs to hear about your company/product at least 12 to 24 times a year, and more often if you're in a cluttered category.

The first impulse for entrepreneurs who spend money on anything that doesn't pay off quickly is to pull the plug. Resist that temptation.

Now and then I hear somebody complain, "We've tried everything—direct mail, advertising, on-line marketing, you name it—but it doesn't work." I ask about frequency and they say, "When we didn't get any response, we decided to pull the plug."

This is like saying to a dentist, "I brushed my teeth a couple of times and still got cavities. I'm not wasting time on *that* anymore."

Consistency

Two factors work against your struggle for consistency. First is the turnover rate among technology marketing people; second is the pace of development in this industry.

Let's start with turnover. Marketing professionals are creative people, and creative people don't like copying somebody else's work. So every time there's a change within your marketing staff, there's potential for your company's message to change.

There's not much you can do about the talent shortage, and there's nothing you can (or should) do to squelch your staff's creative instincts. But you *can* publish crystal-clear elevator and positioning statements, create a graphic standards guide, and require your staff to work from a marketing plan you have personally approved. Establish archives where all of your company's marketing communications—internal, external, print, broadcast, and online—can be reviewed quickly and easily. People reinvent the wheel because they don't know somebody else has already done it.

The second force working against message consistency is the volatility of this industry. Don't modify your message or reposition your company to align with The Next Big Thing. Confusion is deadly when you're trying to build market share and a brand.

Clarity

Clarity and simplicity go hand in hand. Be ruthless about weeding out technobabble and weasel words. Resist the impulse to top your competitors' claims with one more of your own. Define your value proposition simply. Do *not* revamp it every few months and trot it out to the market to see if it catches on.

Focus is the best protection against overcomplicated messages. Choose one market, skill, or product and forsake all others, and you'll be regarded as an authority. People listen carefully when authorities share their expertise, which is an enormous marketing advantage. (There's more about focus in Chapter Three.)

Our brains grasp concrete information 30 percent faster than abstractions. We're wired to reject complexity and to tune out stuff that doesn't compute. These are basic truths about human learning, but one look at the sales materials some tech companies produce makes it clear they haven't heard the news.

Marketing advice from the White House

When people ask, "What do I have to do to be a better communicator?" I give 'em what I call the McCurry Four Cs.

The first is Candor: the ability to speak truthfully and honestly so that you're recognized as somebody who knows the truth and how to tell it. That's probably my biggest lesson from the White House.

The second C is Credibility, which comes in part from candor—being a reliable source of information when you talk about the work you do or the goods and services you sell. That's extremely critical.

Third is Clarity, knowing what you're trying to say and saying it precisely and simply.

The fourth C is Commitment—to telling the story over and over again. You have to persevere.

—Michael McCurry,
Harvard Business Review

THE
COCKTAIL-PARTY TEST

*Can your spouse explain to the neighbors
what you do for a living? Does everybody on
your payroll—including all the salespeople—
describe your business the same way? Do eyes
glaze over when you talk about your company?*

*For many technology entrepreneurs the
answers are no, no, and yes—whether they'll
admit it or not.*

*That's a problem, because conducting any
marketing effort without a clearly articulated
message is a waste of time and money.*

If every person in your firm can't explain in 20 words or less *what* you do, for *whom* you do it, and *why* it matters—in plain English—it's time to write an elevator statement. You need a company description so crisp and clear that a stranger on an elevator understands it before you get to the second floor.

A good elevator statement is 20 words or less and written in conversational English. The words are short, there aren't many adjectives, and no technical jargon or weasel words are allowed.

Weasel words are meaningless, but they sound important. Popular favorites include "customer-driven," "mission-critical," "paradigm," "best practices"…you get the idea. An email I received recently says it all. This is a direct quote:

> *How applications are used (i.e. "application paradigm") is progressing from on-demand transaction reporting and proactive information dissemination to collaborative interaction…The value of e-commerce applications is the enablement of collaboration (defined as mutually beneficial cooperative problem solving and opportunity exploitation) beyond traditional, predefined trading partners to more quickly find new, different, and innovative ways of solving business problems and capturing new business."*

"Sure, that's fine for other companies," you're saying to

yourself. "But we're so specialized! Our markets understand technical language; in fact, they expect it. And they're the only ones who matter."

Think again. Industry outsiders—potential employees, analysts, funding sources, Wall Street, and the media—have an enormous influence on your company. And even subject-matter experts usually respond better to plain English than to jargon.

A good elevator statement, repeated with conviction, will clear the ultimate hurdle—the cocktail-party test—every time. Here's how it works.

Before

The scene:	Cocktail reception at an industry trade show
You:	"Hi! I'm Bill with Complicated Widgitology."
Frank:	"Nice to meet you, Bill. What does Complicated Widgitology do?"
You:	"We're the world-recognized leader in technology, education, and advisory services for strategic balance-sheet management, profitability and performance measurement, and financial accounting." (Note: this description is taken verbatim from an actual corporate Web site.)
Frank:	"Oh. Gotta go. Nicetameetcha."

After

The scene:	Cocktail reception at an industry trade show
You:	"Hi! I'm Bill with Complicated Widgitology."
Frank:	"Nice to meet you, Bill. What does Complicated Widgitology do?"
You:	"Software and services for financial institutions."
Frank:	"Really? Who do you work with?"
You:	"Well, Megawatt Regional Bank is a client of ours. The performance improvement program we designed for them was so successful the bank sold for a multiple of 50."
Frank:	"No kidding! Got a card? Let's talk."

Can anybody really argue against the "after" scenario? You bet. In fact, half the staff at Complicated Widgitology probably can—and will.

Why? Because it's "too simple." It doesn't mention education, balance sheets, accounting, worldwide recognition, motherhood, or apple pie. It leaves out all those "important" things that separate Complicated from its competitors.

Sacred as those attributes are to Complicated Widgitology, someone who's being introduced to the firm doesn't care about them yet. When we say too much too soon, bad things happen. Instead of understanding everything, our listener doesn't understand anything.

At this point you may be thinking, "But if we don't mention it, nobody will know we can do it!" (Your real fear? Losing a business opportunity because you failed to say the magic words.)

You can go into detail later. The goal is to say just enough to pique interest, elicit a question, or spark a comment. When that happens, your listener (or reader) has given you permission to say more.

Several years ago one of the largest companies in the world hired our firm to conduct a messaging workshop for an underperforming division. Up to that point, we'd worked primarily with small and mid-tier companies, so we figured this client would be quite buttoned-up and savvy about sales and marketing.

Boy, were we wrong.

We spent two days in a conference room with their senior management team to hammer out elevator and positioning statements. But it was clear within the first hour that none of the R&D, customer-support, and sales people could agree on their product's benefits, target markets, or competitors—and they *all* disagreed with the division vice-president (although the product had been on the market for three years!)

I was surprised to see confusion about such a basic business issue. This multi-billion-dollar conglomerate seemed to be violating the golden rule of marketing—*consistency above all*—and doing it successfully.

But it only looked that way. Even for this huge company, a good message couldn't save a bad product or a misaligned management team. That's when I realized the power of a brand. Solid-gold brand equity compensated for this firm's mistakes at the individual and divisional levels—but not forever. The troubled division was sold six months later.

Internal confusion doesn't disappear. It magnifies as it reaches the outside world, and once out there it's like a slow leak: hardly noticeable at first, but guaranteed to halt your progress. Find it and fix it early, and adopt a zero-tolerance policy against weasel words, technobabble, and hot air.

How to develop an elevator statement that works

Send the following message to everybody in your firm. *Note to senior executives:* don't delegate this task! You're the only one with enough clout and insight into business objectives to make the exercise successful.

> *We're fine-tuning our marketing and sales messages and I'd like your input. There aren't any right or wrong answers, and don't worry about phrasing, spelling, or grammar. None of that stuff matters! Just fill in the blanks with your own words and send it back to me. No need to include your name unless you want to. Thanks.*
>
> *What does our company do?*_____
> _____

*What market(s) do we serve?*_____

_____

*Who are our three closest competitors?*_____

_____

*Why should buyers choose our product over theirs?*_____

_____

*What single thing do we do better than anybody else?*____

_____

Now answer the following questions, based on your employees'
responses and your own vision for the business. The completed
sentence will be your elevator statement. Limit it to 20 words
or less and keep it completely free of weasel words and hot air.

*Our company provides*_____
    (name your product or service)

*For*_____
        (name your target market)

*So they can*_____
        (describe the problem you help them solve)

Don't be discouraged. This process takes time, concentra-
tion, and commitment. When you have a statement you like,
try it out on employees, your family, and a customer or two. If
they respond with a glassy-eyed stare, go back and try again.
Because when you *do* get it, you'll know it—and so will everybody else.

N O B O D Y   L O V E S
A   N A R C I S S I S T

A cartoon in The New Yorker *a few years ago showed an executive reviewing storyboards with account executives from his ad agency. They're rolling their eyes and he's blustering, "It's MY company, it's MY ad, and I'LL be the one that stars in it!"*

That's too true to be funny. CEOs like Eckhardt Pfeiffer, formerly of Compaq, Larry Ellison of Oracle, and Thomas Seibel of Seibel Systems perpetrate the "just show them my photo and they will come" philosophy. If you're tempted to follow suit, don't.

CEO-centered ads violate the sacred principle of WIIFM— *What's in it for me?* That's the fundamental question human beings ask themselves every minute of every day. If your ad doesn't answer it in six seconds or less, forget it. You might as well spend your marketing budget on floor-to-ceiling mirrors.

Name-dropping is equally annoying. Yes, it's tempting to use your customers, especially those with recognizable names, to build credibility. But testimonials can be confusing if they aren't handled well.

Flipping through three computer magazines turned up the following. If you can figure out at first glance who the advertisers are and what they're selling, you either wrote these ads or paid for them.

> "From $0.0 to $1.8 billion in about a year. Now that I have your attention, I'd like you to meet my investment banker. Volpe took AboveNet to the top at light speed by knowing exactly what to do. When to do it. And how to do it."
>
> —*Warren J. Kaplan, AboveNet Communications, Inc.*
> (*Ad for Volpe Brown Whelan*)

> "DaimlerChrysler chose the world's most powerful CAD/CAM/CAE software. Now smaller manufacturers like Precision Products can make the same choice."
>
> (*Ad for Catia Solutions*)

> "Who helped Alloy Online generate fashion sales from Generation Y?"
>
> (*Ad for OneSoft*)

5

YOUR PERSONA: BLUE CHIP WON'T WORK ANYMORE

- *Ditch that plastic ficus in the lobby*

- *"But what if they don't get it?"*

- *Think twice before renaming your company*

DITCH THAT PLASTIC FICUS IN THE LOBBY

As recently as five or six years ago, clients who came to us for a new corporate identity all wanted the same thing: "Make us look blue-chip. Solid. Like a Fortune 500 company."

Those days are behind us. Today, blue-chip means old. Stodgy. Slow. Traditional. Not the attributes for a 21st-century technology company.

If your logo is as close to IBM's as it can get without landing you in court, your lobby decor is maroon and gray, and your sales presentations take 45 minutes in a darkened room while somebody reads bullet points off a screen, you're out of touch. (As *Fortune* magazine says, "It all screams '*go away!*'")

The only way to win is to play the game *your* way. That means stepping out, speaking out, getting noticed, creating a little controversy now and then. Courage and imagination count, and they start at the front door.

Plenty of entrepreneurs are still convinced that their surroundings are incidental to the success of their businesses. ("If my people have time to stare at the walls, they aren't working hard enough," one told me grumpily.) But 30-and-under employees don't agree. This group simply won't work in a beige rabbit warren if there's any other alternative. And increasingly, there are plenty of alternatives. So if you're struggling to attract, recruit, and retain talent, look around. Does the space you occupy reinforce or undermine the brand you want to build?

If you're stuck with a six-year lease in a suburban office park, you *can* make the environment more appealing. The first step is to walk through your lobby as if you've never seen it before.

Ditch the fake flowers and silk plants. It doesn't matter how expensive they were or who lovingly arranged them, get rid of them. Ditto for the reproduction landscapes. Nude walls are only one step up from that bad art however, so replace the homogenized stuff with something more personal.

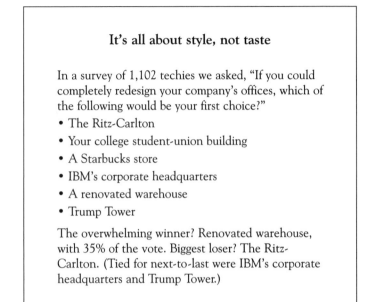

It's all about style, not taste

In a survey of 1,102 techies we asked, "If you could completely redesign your company's offices, which of the following would be your first choice?"
• The Ritz-Carlton
• Your college student-union building
• A Starbucks store
• IBM's corporate headquarters
• A renovated warehouse
• Trump Tower

The overwhelming winner? Renovated warehouse, with 35% of the vote. Biggest loser? The Ritz-Carlton. (Tied for next-to-last were IBM's corporate headquarters and Trump Tower.)

Let your employees' kids—or their brothers and sisters, if you have a very young staff—draw pictures of family at work. Frame the art, hang it in the lobby, and hold an open house to show it off.

Another source for artwork is your local elementary school. Invite a class to visit your firm and paint pictures of what they think you do all day. There's nothing more telling (or more appealing) than a kid's-eye view of the world. Who knows? Some of those students might be your best employees in a few years.

If your walls are gray or '80s mauve, call building maintenance and have them repainted. Throw out the outdated pile of *PC Weeks* and *Interactive Ages* on the coffee table, and if there isn't at least one magazine somebody might actually read in the stack—*Rolling Stone, Fast Company, GQ, Popular Mechanics, Sports Illustrated, anything*—buy one today and put it there.

Smart companies are realizing that their space can reinforce their brand. Office furniture is taking a more casual, less hierarchical approach (so that) the boss's office looks more like the workers' offices. The giant, all-wood, Daddy Warbucks executive power desk and the mahogany "workwall" credenza may become endangered species.

—*The Financial Post*

Make oversized (*really* oversized—four or five times bigger than life) enlargements of customer thank-you letters and deck the halls with them. Paint your lobby vermilion with zebra stripes. Install an exercise bike or a fish pond. Not a fish tank, a fish pond.

Are your marketing people more imaginative than you are? They'd better be. This is true even if you're pretty flamboyant yourself. Your staff and your ad agency should regularly bring you ideas that are a little brasher, a little weirder, a little more out there than you'd ordinarily consider. If they can't work to this standard, get rid of them and hire someone else. (If you've shot these people down in the past when they've attempted to break the mold, give them time to readjust.)

I didn't take the job because I don't own a tie

To get a handle on the issues of employee recruitment and reten-tion, the human resources department surveyed people who had left the company, along with candidates who had turned down job offers. The white-shirt-and-tie culture was less than a hit. Ditto for a workplace filled with rows of cubicles.

—Edward Sullivan, Blueprint for a New Corporate Culture, www.facilitiesnet.com

---

Give these ideas a fair chance, remembering that *some of them will fail.* If Cadillac, the bluehair of the automobile industry, could loosen up enough to promote itself with a cartoon duck, you can certainly take a risk or two.

When's the last time you sat through your company's sales presentation?

Yes, the whole thing.

Imagine Death by Power Point. Even worse, Death by Overhead Projector. All the technical glitz on the planet at our command, and technology people, still give the world's worst presentations. Forbid your staff from reading bullet points to a captive audience. If your first-contact sales presentation doesn't move fast, use plenty of color and examples, and take less than 15 minutes, it's too long. Fix it.

Any business conference should be theatrical in the most positive sense. It should be entertaining, compelling, professional, memorable, and personal, and its first concern should be for the audience.

—*Tom Krattenmaker*, Harvard Management Communication Letter

The most straightlaced business school in the world advises against boring audiences to death. "Passion is something one expects from a performer of music or drama," according to the *Harvard Management Communication Letter*. "But from a business presenter? Absolutely. It doesn't mean you need to shout and weep or leap about the podium. It means communicating the material with conviction, emotion and a natural level of animation."

There you have it—official permission to lighten up.

Maybe you do treasure that desk set engraved with your bank's name, but others are less enthusiastic about gifts bearing somebody else's logo. If you really want to make an impression, personalize a remembrance with their logo.

When it comes to corporate gifts—which don't include promotional items like flashlights, mousepads, and baseball caps—it takes guts to forego your corporate identity. But you'll be regarded more fondly if you give something unusual, fun, or elegant that reflects the recipient rather than yourself.

Everybody wants to have more fun at work

Neither you nor Al Gore should suddenly be Chris Rock or Austin Powers—even if you wanted to. The key to workplace humor is doing what's comfortable. Think about what makes you laugh. Model the behavior of someone whose humor you admire. Just don't make the mistake of assuming that people and organizations either have the knack for fun or don't—and that you don't.

—*David Stauffer,* Harvard Management Update

Do you have a collection of company stories? Nobody forgets a good story. Look for ways to infuse meaning into even the mundane aspects of your business. You can't bore people into remembering who you are, but you sure can intrigue them.

Tom Smith, chairman of Total Technology Ventures, is expert at this. His logo is more than a mark; it's the story of the company. The elements symbolize people, ideas, and goals, and the colors reflect the TTV values. Blue means balance, self-control, and generosity; red represents optimism and vigor; and yellow stands for renewal, liveliness, youth, and audacity.

With the logo as a starting point, Smith brings the company to life powerfully for investors, potential employees, and entrepreneurs. This is the essence of "being your brand."

Whether your firm is six months, 60 months or 60 years old, your corporate history is filled with anecdotes. Pull the best ones out of storage, polish them up and repeat them with pride and conviction. This is how legends are made. *Everybody* wants to be part of a legend.

" B U T   W H A T   I F
T H E Y   D O N ' T   G E T   I T ? "

*Two or three years ago I conducted an
experiment. I sifted through a random stack
of brochures and magazines, clipped a few
paragraphs of copy, eliminated all the company names and had each paragraph blown up
to poster size. These were mounted on boards
and propped up in our conference room.*

*I asked everyone who walked by if they
could tell what businesses these companies
were in. Try it yourself, then check out the
answers below. (In case you're wondering,*

no one has ever guessed any of them correctly.)

Example #1

"Since 1971, _____ has used its expertise to devise integrated systems that help our clients gain new levels of efficiency and productivity. Today, we are an acknowledged leader in the development of technology-based solutions in both the public and private sectors."

Example #2

"_____ prides itself on being a source of significant competitive advantage through its talented work force and advanced technology. _____ can cut costs and provide differentiation in the marketplace while enhancing safety and product security."

Example #3

"_____ strives to ensure that customers reach their optimum operating potential. We focus on developing innovative products to help increase our customers' bottom line. Our commitment stems from a long history of technological leadership, innovative thinking, and industry firsts."

Check out the answers below.

Why do companies fall into this trap? *Because they're afraid of being misunderstood, looking strange, or confusing their customers and prospects.* But ironically, that's exactly what happens. They

#1: Benefits processor for food stamp programs; #2: Automobile tires; #3: Rental trucks

say so much that they communicate nothing, and they look and sound just like everybody else.

Cynical art directors have a standing joke about good, but unusual, concepts that die on the conference table. "If the client says, 'but what if they don't get it?' you *know* it's good stuff."

Young companies like to emulate the market leader, but resist this temptation. Break the mold. You've got absolutely nothing to lose and everything to gain.

I'm not advocating weird ideas solely for shock value, nor am I promoting advertising that trivializes your product, your company, or your customer. I am urging you to have the courage to speak up, speak clearly, and express your message in your own voice. They'll get it.

T H I N K   T W I C E
B E F O R E   R E N A M I N G
Y O U R   C O M P A N Y

There are lots of thankless marketing jobs in the world, but renaming your company ranks right up there at the top.

If you're considering a corporate name change, be prepared for a rash of unsolicited opinions, political maneuvering, and frustration. And keep in mind that no matter what the final result may be, somebody's not going to like it.

Naming a company or a product is exactly

like naming a child. It's no big deal to anybody but the immediate family but, boy, does that family have strong opinions. In the world outside, some will like the name you chose for the kid and some won't, but most won't give it a second thought.

When I was working for corporate America, the two issues almost guaranteed to bring senior management to blows were (1) product names, and (2) product colors. Everything else, they were willing to leave to the engineers...

—Stephen Fleming, Alliance Technology Ventures

The acid tests for a good company or product name are quite simple. Is it memorable? Will it translate into other languages or shorten to an acronym without embarrassment? Can you protect it legally? If the answer to any of these questions is "no," keep looking. The most unusual, descriptive, elegant name in the world is useless if people can't remember it or somebody else owns it.

If you're determined to do it, here's how

Most companies follow one of two paths. They throw the process open to employees, usually offering a prize for the winning suggestion, or they hire an ad agency or naming consultant right off the bat. If one approach doesn't work, they switch gears and try the other. Neither is guaranteed to produce results immediately, and there are pros and cons to each tactic.

Inviting employees to get involved is a great idea on the face of it. It builds camaraderie and is far less expensive than hiring an outsider. You can offer a handsome reward for the winning name—$2,000 isn't out of the question and certainly less than you'll spend on an outside resource. But how will you break the news if you don't like anything they recommend?

You'll face the same problem in reverse if the contest yields several readily available good names. Who gets the prize? In this happy (though unlikely) scenario, it's up to you to make the final decision. Do *not* leave it up to a vote.

Buying outside help

If you decide to hire professionals to help find a new name, there are several ways to go about it. There's the collaborative approach, when a naming consultant or an ad agency facilitates working sessions where you and your colleagues take an active part in brainstorming. There's also the hands-off alternative, where the consultant researches and presents recommendations for you to simply review and approve (or reject).

I've been involved in all these scenarios. In my experience all are cumbersome and none are foolproof, but the collaborative technique works better than any of the others.

Why? The employee free-for-all has too many political pitfalls, and executives who delegate the task completely drive themselves—and the agency—crazy with interminable trips back to the drawing board. If you're not personally involved in what goes on behind the scenes, it's too easy to reject ideas with the flick of a pen. You suspect the agency's just running up billable hours ("It's only a name, for crying out loud. Don't you people do this every day?") while the agency becomes discouraged about not being able to please you.

Never delegate this task completely. You'll wind up feeling ripped off. *Why did it cost so much and take so long to find a name I could have come up with myself?*

It's possible you will feel that way even when you *do* take a more active role. (I told you this is a thankless job.) You may collaborate with an outside resource for weeks or months, only to wind up settling on a name you came up with all by yourself. Why should you write a check for somewhere between $3,000 and $50,000?

Because you're paying for time and ideas, not guarantees. Don't hire outside help unless you're both committed to a mutual goal: working together to find a memorable, protectable name, regardless of its source.

What to expect in a naming session

Agencies and naming consultants all have their own techniques, but collaborative sessions share certain characteristics. The groups aren't large: five or six participants from your company plus a facilitator and a scribe from the agency.

Unwieldy committees don't work. Keep the list short, even though you'll be tempted to add "just one more person."

It's best to meet off-site. Go to your agency's offices or a third-party location. Turn the pagers and cell phones off. Even better, leave them at home. The meeting room will be stocked with flip charts, white boards, Post-It® notes, felt pens, a thesaurus, a dictionary, and a computer with Internet access. It's possible you'll also have a supply of crayons, colored pens, construction paper, and toys. This is a creative process, and the more imaginative you allow yourself to be, the better you'll like the results.

The facilitator will kick off by clarifying expectations (what's possible? what isn't?) and giving you a rundown on how his or her brainstorming process works. If you briefed the agency people ahead of time, they may have conducted competitive and creative research and developed a list of 25 to 100 possible names. This list is a working document, the launching point for brainstorming. Other facilitators like to start with a clean slate, generating all ideas within the group.

You'll spend the next few hours on activities that produce thousands of words, non-words, phrases, and ideas. Since very few people can sustain creative energy for more than five or six hours at a stretch, it's most productive to schedule two half-day sessions at least 24 hours apart. If the group hits the jackpot on the first day, great: you can go home early. Just don't count on it.

Ultimately you will boil this hodgepodge down to about 50

names, each segmented into first-, second-, and third-choice categories. If you haven't been doing it all along, go online now to see which names are available. (Check them out at www.register.com or any of the other trademark databases.) In most cases the winner will emerge by default: it's the name closest to the top of the list that's still available as a URL.

Avoid these naming traps!

Don't invite everybody to participate in brainstorming. Involving more than six people from your company changes the group dynamic. (In fact, many experienced facilitators draw the line at five.) The agency or consultant will probably have no more than two representatives involved, with only one of them playing an active part. The other takes notes and handles online availability checks.

Don't strive for consensus. People will polarize as the brainstorming session wears on. A skilled facilitator keeps the discussion moving without forcing a conclusion, because premature decisions never stick. As the senior executive, the right—and the responsibility—to break a logjam is yours.

This isn't always a comfortable role, but I've observed that even the most mild-mannered entrepreneurs have strong opinions about the company name, whether or not they express it. They *always* find a way, consciously or unconsciously, to get the outcome they want. This is not a bad thing, it's just a fact. Don't wait for the group to struggle toward consensus. It won't happen. Make an executive decision and move on.

Don't settle for mush just because it's easier. The days of naming tech companies "Total Impact Solutions" and "Quality Technology Services" are over. (Well, maybe not; but they should be.) You owe it to your company, your employees and your customers to come up with something more than a string of meaningless weasel words.

Real or invented words are 40% easier to remember than all-initial names. Don't believe that? Try this little test. Below are pairs of company names taken right out of the Fortune 500 listings. The names are side by side in the tables, just one ranking apart. Which half of each pair is better known? Which is easier to identify? (Be honest.) LTV or MicroAge? GPU or Foster Wheeler? USF&G or Maytag? USG or New York Times Co.?

—The Naming Newsletter, Rivkin & Associates

You'll get discouraged during your name search, but don't give in to cliches. Loosen up a little and you'll discover a whole world of good ideas. Purple Rain, for example, is a much better company name than Advanced Communications Technologies. Neither one describes the business you're in—but one's certainly a lot more memorable. (No, I am not advocating meaningless flash-in-the-pan names. But you get the idea.)

Don't force linear thinking while you're brainstorming. Ninety percent of what goes on in a brainstorming session is junk. But it is absolutely necessary junk. Avoid becoming impatient with stalled-out processes or ideas that seem to go nowhere. I've seen marathon brainstorming sessions where nothing seemed to happen until the last five minutes—when "suddenly" a good solution appeared.

The best way to ensure a good outcome is to work with a knowledgeable facilitator and stick with the process until you accomplish the goal. ("Knowledgeable facilitator" are the key words here. Wading through committee naming sessions is difficult, if not impossible, without an objective outside guide.)

Don't expect the facilitator to do all the work. Sooner or later—usually during the fourth or fifth hour—every brainstorming session quits being fun and turns into a grind. At that point it's easy to sit back in your chair and think, *Why am I working so hard? The agency's being paid to come up with something. Let them take it from here.* Tempting, but fatal. Abdicating the responsibility won't work. You're in this together.

Remember the old saw, "The darkest hour's just before dawn?" This is true both literally and metaphorically. There are three steps in the naming process: cliché, chaos, and true creativity. *Everyone* is tempted to throw in the towel during the chaos stage, often just inches before they break through to a creative discovery. They never realize how close they are.

Don't be afraid your company will fail if you choose the wrong name. Businesses are like people: no name in the world can guarantee success or failure. Don't be buffaloed by "experts" who say the future of your company hangs upon the perfect name. A good name? Yes. The perfect name? It doesn't exist.

In truth, a bad or innocuous name is a liability and a good name is an asset, but it's the brand you build behind the name that counts. After all, given a choice, would *you* name a company IBM?

Until you're sure the name you've chosen is available, keep several in play. If you make a premature commitment and your favorite name is already taken, it is extremely difficult to refocus and reenergize your company to go through the whole process again.

—*Upside Today*

Don't fall in love with a name you can't have. Rule out conflicts *before* you get attached to a name. I remember one grueling, eight-hour session where the group finally settled on a dozen possibilities. Nobody thought to do domain name checks during the course of the day. At five o'clock, when everyone was cranky and brain-dead, somebody pulled out a laptop and logged onto a naming database.

Not one of their 12 choices was available. The letdown was awful, and got worse as they dug deeper into their second- and third-choice categories. The name that finally cleared was a very good one (stronger, in fact, than anything on the first list) but getting there was more difficult than it had to be.

Asking for opinions: two schools of thought

Okay, you've chosen a name. Should you test your choice before you officially announce it? "Testing" means anything from running the name past a few customers to conducting a full-fledged focus group.

I don't recommend this. Why? For the same reason I didn't ask outsiders what to call my kids. What if my mother-in-law hated the names Bridgitt and Alexandra and suggested Ottolina and Figby instead? Asking for advice implies that you'll take it, so you'd better be careful what you ask for.

Soliciting *any* outside opinion (attorneys and foreign-language translators excepted) simply prolongs the process and confuses the issue. We suggest that our clients check legal and Internet availability, make sure the name doesn't suffer when it's translated or abbreviated, make a decision, and stick to it.

Not everyone's comfortable with this unilateral approach. If you fall into this camp, print out your final name choices in 72-point type and fax them to a few customers and influencers. Ask them to rank their favorites in priority order. What you do with this information is up to you.

When does a corporate name change make sense?

- When a change of ownership stipulates a legal name change

- When your existing name can't be trademarked or isn't available as a URL

- When you're rebuilding after trauma: bankruptcy, scandal

- When there's confusion in the market (multiple firms with similar names)

- When you're spinning off or launching an independent entity

- When you become part of a big-name firm and can bask in the halo effect

- When you've changed focus and the old name reflects the old business

When is a corporate name change a bad idea?

- When it's just an ego trip in disguise

- When the new CEO wants the old CEO's name off the door

- When the ad agency says you need to update your identity because…well, just because

- When a consultant tells you it's the only way to go

- When the boss's spouse complains about the existing name but nobody else does

104   *Useful naming resources*

www.uspto.gov is the U.S. Patent and Trademark Office site, where you can check online for trademark conflicts. The database is updated quarterly.

www.register.com is one of many online databases updated daily, weekly, or monthly. Find others by typing "trademark search" into any search engine.

www.namingnewsletter.com is published by Rivkin & Associates. This is an invaluable resource for anyone charged with naming and renaming products or companies.

6

YOUR AGENCY: HOW TO BE A SMART CLIENT

- *How to hire an ad agency*
- *How to work with an ad agency*
- *How to fire an ad agency*
- *How to build a really bad ad*
- *If your spouse went to art school, keep quiet about it*

How To Hire
An Ad Agency

Agencies differ in their expertise and the services they offer, and the good ones don't try to be everything to everybody.

Generally speaking, there's a great divide between consumer and business-to-business agencies. Don't waste time visiting a firm that has made its reputation promoting off-the-shelf software if you're selling back-office B2B systems. Likewise, if online promotion is critical to your marketing strategy, hiring a company with a print and broadcast portfolio is a risky move.

Don't hire an agency prematurely. It's frustrating and costly for both sides. The wrong firm can be a startup tech company's worst nightmare and vice versa—and mismatches that aren't caught and ended quickly can literally drive one or the other out of business.

Why? "Virgin" clients expect agencies to be infallible. They think marketing should compensate for failings in their product or their sales force, and their expectations about money and ROI are often wildly unrealistic. More than one demanding client has gobbled up an agency's resources—time, ideas, out-of-pocket expenses for subcontractors and media space—then couldn't, or wouldn't, pay the bill, forcing the agency to close its doors or limp through years of reconstruction. The same thing happens when an agency burns through a small company's marketing budget and asks for more.

If neither you nor anyone on your senior staff has ever hired or managed an agency, start smaller. Hire an experienced marketing consultant. Consultants have relationships with creative people—graphic designers and copywriters—and serve as the general contractors for a variety of projects, from strategic planning to creating and placing ads.

Look for a consultant whose chemistry clicks with yours and for whom your company will be a key client. When you outgrow your consultant's bandwidth, you'll be a wiser buyer of agency services.

Never hire an agency until you're convinced it can do

something you can't. You know your products inside and out. You've got a vision for your company and strong opinions about how to get there. You've made the firm what it is today. But until you're convinced the agency knows best when it comes to customer behavior, keep your wallet in your pocket.

Experienced agency people can tell when you're not ready to trust someone else's marketing abilities. It's revealed in your tone of voice, your offhand comments, and your track record (our radar goes off if you're an agency-hopper). Until you believe it can do its job better than you can, you won't be satisfied with any agency's work.

Don't ask for speculative work or an elaborate dog-and-pony show. Some agencies will pull out all the stops for new business, but many won't. At this writing, tech agencies in San Francisco are turning down 200 potential clients for every one they accept. This seller's market won't last, of course, but it *has* forced a healthy change in the pitch process. Agencies that formerly spent thousands of dollars on spec work don't anymore. The expectation is that the portfolio and the people will speak for themselves.

Don't decide in haste. Young agencies are flattered when a prospect says, "Where do I sign?" at the first meeting, but I've learned to be wary of snap decisions. Visit more than one shop before you make a final choice. Chemistry is critical, and so is capability. You can't judge either one in a single meeting.

This doesn't mean you should draw out the decision past the point of common sense. Some companies do arduous tours of six to ten firms, boil down a short list, agonize over the list, return to each agency and ask for spec work, then agonize some more. This is a red flag to the firms you're interviewing. It says you gather endless data before making a decision, and you'll probably do the same as a client.

Don't delegate the decision unless you delegate the authority, too. Smart clients bring top management into the agency selection process just before the final round. We've participated in pitches where the CEO, president, vice president of sales, senior VP of operations, director of marketing, and marketing communications manager were all present. When agency people and line managers can meet face-to-face, everyone's invested in the success of the relationship.

This does not mean the decision should be made by consensus. If you're not making the final choice yourself, assign the responsibility to one person and give him/her complete authority.

Don't go in unprepared. Ask the firms you're considering about their capabilities and experience *before* you show up for the first meeting. This can range from a full-fledged RFP to a one-page list of short questions.

What should you look for in an agency?

Chemistry. Without this, nothing works. There will be trying times in your relationship, and unless you like each other, you won't weather them.

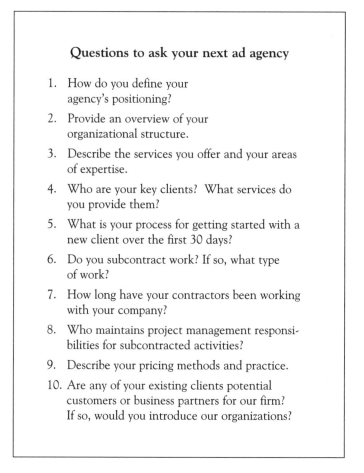

Questions to ask your next ad agency

1. How do you define your agency's positioning?

2. Provide an overview of your organizational structure.

3. Describe the services you offer and your areas of expertise.

4. Who are your key clients? What services do you provide them?

5. What is your process for getting started with a new client over the first 30 days?

6. Do you subcontract work? If so, what type of work?

7. How long have your contractors been working with your company?

8. Who maintains project management responsibilities for subcontracted activities?

9. Describe your pricing methods and practice.

10. Are any of your existing clients potential customers or business partners for our firm? If so, would you introduce our organizations?

Capability. The firm you choose should know your business/market or have expertise in a market you *want* to penetrate. If you're a B2B marketer and you choose an agency with an all-consumer portfolio, be prepared for a steep learning curve (particularly with copywriters) and a lot of education on your dollar.

Make sure the agency you choose has depth and breadth in the non-advertising areas that matter to you. We've presented clients' marketing plans to their investors, trained their marketing staffs to qualify inquiries, and met with their prospects to learn how the sales presentation could be improved. If you want your agency to go beyond the traditional deliverables, say so. Not everybody can or will take these on. Ask first!

Compatibility. This refers to size, values, and approach to the work. If you're the agency's smallest account, you simply won't get the attention you would at another firm. On the other hand, if your account is their primary source of revenue, both firms are exposed. Your values and approach to the work need to synch up, too, or you'll continually be at odds about deadlines, payment, staffing, and supplier issues.

Connections. This really matters in the technology community. The right agency can hook you up with people it could take years to meet otherwise: potential customers, business partners, funding sources, and industry influencers.

Depth. If you choose a "Rolodex" agency (one that depends on freelancers for the creative work), you're likely to experience sporadic quality and a learning curve that never seems to flatten out. Some agencies have conquered this problem and produce consistently great work, but they're the exception rather than the rule. Find out what's handled in-house and what's subcontracted out.

Enthusiasm. Don't settle for an agency that expresses anything less than a genuine interest in your product and the prospect of working with you.

Facts of life about the agency business

No matter what they say, no agency is good at everything. Finding a firm with equal strengths in PR and advertising/sales promotion, for example, is very difficult. You're better off with a couple of boutiques than a big name that claims all powerfulness or a second-tier shop that does both in a mediocre fashion. Be careful, too, about getting carried away with the creative product and not inquiring about strategy. If you expect your agency to have marketing smarts (and not all do), ask for proof.

Personnel churn is a sore spot for agencies and clients alike. Turnover ranges from 15% to 30% for agencies specializing in technology accounts. The job calls for a rare combination of a passion for technology, stellar communications skills, and the ability to work with all sorts of personalities under intense deadline pressure. Once recruited, hired, and trained, good people are often lured away to the client side for more money and options. Don't be surprised if your agency agreement includes an anti-raid clause.

Expect to pay a monthly retainer. Mid-sized and large firms usually work on a retainer basis (a set spending level each month) rather than project by project. Retainers allow the firm to predict the workload and guarantee service levels by staffing accordingly.

Good agencies think they're choosing you. There's a saying in this business: "We get the clients we deserve." As you evaluate agencies, keep in mind that you're being evaluated, too. Expect to be asked about your vision for your company, your product's competitive environment, your business model, and your track record. Most agencies will pull your D&B report and call around for references before accepting you as a client. You may also be asked to pre-pay a percentage of the project cost before the work begins, at least initially. Don't take this personally: many agencies pre-bill all clients as a matter of policy.

How To Work
With An Ad Agency

There isn't much an agency won't do for its favorite client. We'll stay up until all hours to meet impossible deadlines, we'll deliver more than you pay for, we'll give you our very best work and then some, and we'll feel privileged to do it. Here's how to become your agency's favorite account.

Stay in the loop. Don't disappear after you've made your agency selection. Your staff people may be our primary day-to-day contacts, but your presence at appropriate times is both welcome and necessary.

Request regular updates in person. Ask your senior agency representative for face-to-face briefings at regular intervals: monthly, quarterly, semiannually. You'll learn more in a ten minute meeting than you will from a hundred pages of contact reports.

Don't hoard information. Strategies, changes, and news are crucial to your marketing efforts. Share them. If you're too busy to download timely information, that's a problem. Figure out how to solve it.

Are you a marketing cynic?

Phrases to avoid when working with your agency:

- "Corporate brochures? Ads? Nobody reads that stuff."
- "This product's so good it'll sell itself."
- "We just need to get out there, make a splash, you know…"
- "Our business is complicated. You have to be an insider to really understand it."

Fix your internal communication problems. Don't use the agency as a scapegoat for internal dysfunction. Are your objectives measurable? Are your expectations clear? Is communication about the relationship—both the bad and the good—delivered consistently and even-handedly? Errors, chronically missed deadlines, budget overruns, and personality clashes are seldom one-sided. Get to the heart of the issue and fix it—whether the problem is internal, external, or both.

Where do technology clients miss the boat?

They don't push agencies hard enough. They need to challenge their strategic assumptions and ensure they understand the business.

They don't give agencies enough creative leeway and often produce "advertising by committee": generally a committee of left-brain, linear-thinking programmers.

They don't commit sufficient media funds to achieve a meaningful share of voice. Too many times campaigns get cut after two months.

—*Ralph Fascitelli, CEO, Imagio/JWT*

Give the agency access to people who know things. This includes your customers, dealers, business partners, and field employees. Agency people who are cut off from your business turn into order-takers, and that's a terrible way to spend your money.

Pick up the phone and say "thanks" now and then. A client once told me, "I don't praise your people because I don't want our rates to go up." He wasn't kidding.

Pay your bills on time. There's nothing more demeaning than doing your best for someone, then begging to get paid.

Visit our offices now and then. Many behind-the-scenes agency people never meet the clients they serve. You're a VIP to everyone in the firm, and seeing you in person is a treat. Visit your agency just to say hello.

Allow enough time to do the work right. This business is built on speed and urgency, and every agency pulls all-nighters to meet tight deadlines. But when everything is an emergency, our enthusiasm fades. It's worse when you ask for a miracle, then complain about how much it costs.

How To Fire
An Ad Agency

Firing your agency is just like terminating an employee: if it's a surprise, it has been mishandled. Go directly to the agency principal with the problem, give the firm a fair opportunity to remedy the situation, and if it doesn't improve pay your bill and move on.

There are at least four reasons to let your agency go. Each of these situations has warning signs, and none of them crop up overnight:

- One firm has outgrown the other
- Recurring performance problems
- Poor chemistry at multiple levels
- Financial mismanagement

One firm has outgrown the other. This means your company needs services your agency cannot provide or your agency can no longer serve you profitably.

If you need additional talent or services and want to continue the relationship, talk to the principal directly. The agency may be in a position to add the resource, especially since there's a client ready and waiting to pay for it. (You're not obligating yourself to a long-term situation here. It's up to the agency to find additional ways to make the new service profitable.)

If the firm does gear up to meet your needs, expect a learning curve. It's worth hanging in there because you've got a very committed supplier. If the agency can't, or won't, add the resources you need, expect a gracious handoff to a new agency.

If the situation is reversed and your agency outgrows you, the company will attempt to maintain the status quo as long as possible. Agency people are relationship people, and we hate to see relationships end. But an ethical principal will tell you when he/she can no longer serve you and will make the handoff to a new firm easy and painless. Your current agency is a good source of recommendations for other firms that might be a good fit.

Recurring performance problems. The key word here is "recurring." When the same mistakes crop up over and over again, there's an 80% chance that the problem is a procedural rather than a personnel issue. It could be within your organization, within the agency, or both.

Before firing your staff, the agency, or anybody else, your first obligation is to check out what's happening at your end and advise the person running your agency to do the same.

This doesn't mean *asking* people what's happening—it means *seeing for yourself* what's happening.

Yes, I realize how busy you are. I know you're paying other people to solve these problems. But it's your problem, and it will get worse until you see firsthand how the communication flows in and out of your company. With so many people involved in the agency-client dialogue, key information falls through the cracks at dozens of points.

An irate systems integrator told me, "We've spent half a million dollars on marketing this year and haven't closed a single deal. Heads are going to roll." He had a new corporate identity, sales literature, a Web site, case studies, and advertising and direct-mail campaigns, but wasn't seeing any sales results. Upon closer investigation, it turns out that no one was following up on inquiries. The sales force thought it was the agency's job, but this was news to the agency. Potential business dried up in somebody's in-box.

If the performance problem isn't procedural, ask yourself three questions. First, have you given the agency time to learn your business? Even companies familiar with your space need

30 to 90 days to ramp up; others will take considerably longer. Second, are you positive that they're getting accurate, complete information? Third, do you know they have timely access to the right people within your organization? If you can answer yes to all three, there's only one conclusion. The agency just doesn't get it. Your product, your market, or your business are beyond them. You can educate them on your dollar or find another firm.

Poor chemistry at multiple levels. It's hard enough to maintain a long-term relationship with somebody you like. It's practically impossible with somebody you *don't* like. And frankly, why should you? Every business has its share of annoying people, and it's inevitable that you'll run into a few now and then. But if the agency person you work with irritates you, ask for another account person. (This is true even if you're dealing with the principal.) If the agency doesn't have enough bench strength to make a switch, ask yourself if starting all over again with another firm is worth it. If the answer is yes, do so.

What if the chemistry problem isn't isolated to one person? Failures to click one-on-one can be solved, but broad incompatibility means your firms' cultures, values, or style are so far apart that you need to move on. Before you do this, be certain the problems you're experiencing aren't based on petty jealousy or fear. The agency is the first scapegoat for internal difficulties, particularly when the client's marketing people are over their heads.

Every profession has its prima donnas. Agencies and technology companies are no exception. Prima donnas are bullies, and they poison good working relationships. You'll pay heavily for tolerating this behavior and the price is seldom worth it. Among the warning signs:

- Prima donnas are convinced there's only one right answer to a problem: theirs. They focus on a single solution, usually very tightly worked out.

- They interpret comments or questions as disagreement.

- They resort to generalizations: "We've always done it this way, and it's always worked before."

- They view middle ground as compromise, and compromise is bad.

- They're poor listeners.

- Eye contact falls off when conflict arises.

- In tense situations they become petulant, flippant, or patronizing.

- They resolve conflict by abdicating responsibility ("Fine, do it your way! But don't say I didn't warn you") or walking out.

Financial mismanagement. Your agency's financial stability can have a direct impact on your own. Firms that operate on a shoestring sometimes use client media dollars to fund operations, and when the media bill is due they can't pay it. You are responsible for the debt if you have signed a sequential liability agreement. Perform your due diligence up front.

How can you tell when your agency's getting ready to fire *you*? Once again, there are always warning signs. Agencies resign accounts when:

- Clients don't pay their bills
- Clients don't listen to the agency's advice
- Everything's a fight
- The client's staff is hard to reach and access to senior people is blocked
- The client has misled the agency about the company or the product
- There's constant disagreement within the client organization about strategy, structure, and goals

What to do before you drop the ax

"Agencies are generally fired not for poor performance but for poor communication. If you're a concerned client, ask your agency for a review summarizing objectives, strategies, work to date, and challenges. If you're not satisfied, ask the agency to come back with suggested remedies and a timetable. If the goals aren't met at the end of that schedule, you're justified in firing."

"We've resigned accounts that don't pay their bills on a timely basis or don't respect the marketing function or the agency's input. We've never resigned, however, to take on a bigger/better piece of competitive business. Agencies are surprisingly loyal to good clients."

—Ralph Fascitelli, CEO, Imagio/JWT

How To Build A Really Bad Ad

1. *Kick things off with a big meeting. The more opinions the better. It's helpful to have your agency people there, but if they aren't, somebody can fill them in later.*

2. *Pick a strategy. Example: "Whatever we do, it's gotta be better than that crappy ad Bigdeal Systems ran in InfoWorld last month."*

3. *Brainstorm. What you want is a concept—a "big idea." Baby at keyboard?*

Coworkers at conference table? Piece o' cake! Why do agencies think this is so tough?

4. Be practical. You know your buyers, and if the ad's too "different" they just won't get it.

5. Give the agency a couple of hours to come up with draft copy and a layout. They'll want more time, but how long can a picture and a couple of paragraphs take, anyway?

6. Route the layout around for review. Send it to everybody on the management committee, and don't forget your wife, your assistant, and the receptionist. Run it past a couple of customers, too.

7. Email everybody's comments and criticisms to the agency. Don't worry if the edits contradict each other— the account executive will figure it out.

8. Don't be surprised if the agency people get a little snappish as the revision cycles pile up. Thousands— maybe millions—of people will see this ad, so it has to be absolutely perfect. (And don't forget who's paying the bills.)

9. Measure the results. If the ad pulls a pretty good response, call it a success. If it doesn't, call the agency and tell them to do a better job next time.

IF YOUR SPOUSE WENT TO ART SCHOOL, KEEP QUIET ABOUT IT

Here's the scene. You've sweated for months over an acquisition plan, and now you're presenting it to the board. The premise is solid, but one of your board members doesn't seem to be buying it.

Finally he speaks up. "The guy I play tennis with thinks this technology you're looking at is on its last legs. Let's run it by him before you go any further."

Months of work swirl down the drain. This guy doesn't know squat, but he's got enough clout to delay, or derail, the whole project. Forget the launch schedule; your hands are full just keeping the idea alive. Meanwhile, the business opportunity sits there waiting to be claimed.

Looking back, I'd still pick most of my clients, because they gave us the freedom to knock the walls down. And I know there are other clients like them. Treasure these people. They are heroes of great work.

—Phil Dusenberry, Chairman, BBDO New York

Now think back to those concept meetings with your ad agency and marketing staff. What's your initial reaction when you see work in process?

Is it anything like, "I hate orange. And what in the world are these circles supposed to mean?" Or, "I think I'll run these by my wife. She went to art school and she's got a good eye for this stuff"?

If you want to kill any idea in the world, get a committee working on it.

—Charles Kettering

Hire professionals and stand back

To earn the respect of any creative team, give them enough clear direction to succeed and enough leeway to experiment. I guarantee you'll get their best work. A few rules of thumb:

Reject clichés. Everybody's seen that irritating handshake photo a thousand times. And how many 8 1/2" x 11" brochures crossed your desk last month?

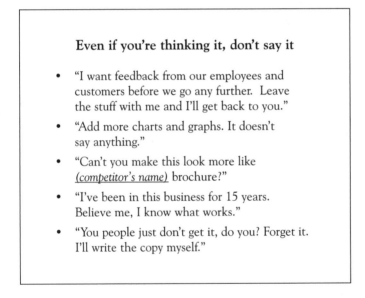

Even if you're thinking it, don't say it

- "I want feedback from our employees and customers before we go any further. Leave the stuff with me and I'll get back to you."
- "Add more charts and graphs. It doesn't say anything."
- "Can't you make this look more like *(competitor's name)* brochure?"
- "I've been in this business for 15 years. Believe me, I know what works."
- "You people just don't get it, do you? Forget it. I'll write the copy myself."

Don't mistake white space for wasted space. It draws attention to what is on the page and improves readership.

134   *It's impossible to please everyone.* Don't try.

Don't over-analyze. The more you pick at a creative approach, the faster the glow wears off and the less you'll like it. No one will spend as much time examining your marketing materials as you will.

Don't lapse into generalizations. There's no right or wrong approach for any particular audience. Engineers and technical people don't always respond best to toned-down visuals and long copy. Give your audience creative credit.

Don't be timid about supporting good advertising. When you pay for professional marketing counsel, protect your investment. Don't be middle-of-the-road on the finished product, and don't make approvals a group activity. The test of an ad or a piece of collateral isn't whether you like it. It's whether the audience saw it, remembered it, and did something as a result.

7

MONEY: THE MOMENT OF TRUTH

- *"They never give us a straight answer about money."*
- *Half your marketing budget goes down the drain.*

  Here's how to get it back

"They Never Give Us A Straight Answer About Money."

Money problems can ruin even the best relationships, and agencies and clients are no exception. Sadly, I don't know if the under-current of suspicion (Are they taking advantage of me?) ever goes away com-pletely. But I do know that unless both sides are realistic about budgets and costs, the relationship turns real ugly, real fast.

The gist of this chapter is to demystify some of the financial issues that surround marketing. But first, I'm going to give you an inside look at how agencies make and lose money. Hopefully, a peek behind the curtain will lend some perspective to the classic accusation agencies and clients make about each other: *"They never give us a straight answer about money."*

Client: *"How much will it cost?"*

Agency: *"How much have you got? Just take that number and double it."*

—How entrepreneurs interpret budget discussions with an ad agency

---

During your first meeting with an ad agency, the people on the other side of the table will slot you into one of two categories—novice or seasoned client—based on the first few questions you ask. If you're a novice, you immediately want to know what stuff costs.

Agencies that aren't interested in missionary work will decide right then and there to decline your business. Why? Your first priority is getting the answer to a question that simply can't be answered on the spot—but odds are you won't believe it when we tell you that.

You're thinking, *"Yeah, right. If this agency really has launched 200 products over the last 14 years, why won't these guys come right out and tell me what it's going to cost?"*

Agencies don't operate like car dealers. We aren't hiding

the wholesale price somewhere and hoping you won't find out about it, and we're not being evasive when we turn right around and answer your question with one of our own: "What's your budget?"

Marketing? You spend and you spend, and you feel like you're getting nothing for it. But you can't be a player without it.

—Mike Landman, Third Wave Technology Services

It's time to debunk a few myths about ad agencies and money.

Myth #1: If I reveal my budget too soon, the agency will take advantage of me. Baloney. Withholding information about your budget is a waste of your time and ours. The most bizarre reason a potential client ever gave me for not disclosing his budget was this: "If I tell you how much we have, you'll want to spend it all."

Some clients don't like revealing their budget because they're embarrassed about how small it is, so they want to convince the agency to work with them first. This only leaves the agency feeling manipulated. We all have a point below which we can't serve an account profitably, and most of us will tell you right up front what it is. The size of your budget has nothing to do with your personal worth or the viability of your business proposition.

Myth #2: Ad agencies are obscenely profitable, so they can afford to take a chance on me. The average pre-tax profit for top-performing mid-sized agencies in the U.S is 13.3%. Even one or two slow-paying or non-paying clients can have a serious impact on an agency's financial health.

Myth #3: We don't have a budget. It's astonishing how many people say this and really believe it. They may not have a formal budget, but whether they realize it or not, they sure do have a spending threshold. If the agency creates a zero-based proposal in good faith and violates that threshold, the immediate response is, "It costs *how* much? You know we can't afford that!" Presto: hours of work down the drain, and we'll never get that time back.

Myth #4: I can get the same work somewhere else for half the price. No matter what "the work" is, you can get it done elsewhere for half the price. In fact, you *can* probably get it done for a tenth of the price. The key words here are "the same work."

Myth #5: We can do it for less in-house. Actually, this isn't a myth at all. Staffing up internally to handle recurring marketing projects makes sense, and you'll pay less for the work over the long haul. Companies get into trouble when they hire creative people who are motivated by challenge and variety, then are expected to design brochures and update the Web site month after month. The turnover costs will kill you.

Myth #6: Agencies inflate their estimates because they expect us to negotiate. *If we don't push back on their proposals, we're leaving money on the table.* Some firms probably do pad their proposals. But the thrill of negotiating is lost on most agencies: we're paid for our time and our ideas, and the longer it takes to get an estimate approved, the less time we have to do the work. Don't nickel-and-dime estimates just out of principle. If you think there's too much slop in the proposals, talk directly to the senior person in the firm.

Myth #7: Offering a piece of the company in exchange for a discounted rate will make my business more appealing to a first-tier agency. That may have been true a year ago, but it isn't anymore. Every firm has a different policy on this, but those who've been burned were quick to warn their colleagues.

The bad news about budgets

Setting a marketing/advertising budget may be one of the most subjective, frustrating business processes you'll ever face. Whether they'll admit it or not, most firms patch together a loose formula based on past and projected sales data, the company's current financial situation, and the CEO's or CFO's mood at the time.

For privately held software companies with revenues in the $2 million to $10 million range, marketing costs (salaries, overhead, and programs) account for roughly 7% to 10% of total expenses, with the fastest-growing companies at the top end of the range. Superachievers spend even more: the

January 2000 issue of *Software Success* describes a $5 million firm with a 62% profit margin—five times the industry median—that allocates 18% of its budget to marketing.

In theory, there are all sorts of complicated ways to figure out how much you should spend on marketing. Academics label them as follows: percentage of sales (past and forecast), objective and task, competitive matching, break-even analyses, test markets, models of market response, arbitrary, and affordable (I love these last two).

Forget the academics. Let common sense drive your spending decisions. In your company's early life you'll face at least four different marketing challenges, each with different cash demands. How you shift money around to cover them will affect your business profoundly, for better or for worse.

Here's where your marketing dollars must go. By the way, none of these (with the possible exception of the fourth item on the list), are optional.

- Brand-building grows market share over time, but won't generate immediate revenues.

- Promotion delivers short-term sales boosts, but at reduced margins.

- Lead generation/qualification establishes the sales pipeline, but the returns lag expenditures.

- Unseating a competitor is expensive and risky, but sometimes the only route to market domination.

- A new-product launch involves all
  of the above.

As you mull over how to rob Peter to pay Paul, don't feel guilty if you take a completely non-scientific approach. Survey after survey shows that managers—including Harvard MBAs at blue-chip companies all over America—fall back on rules of thumb when they're deciding how much to dump into the marketing pot.

One thing's certain: no matter what the number ends up being, the finance people will think it's too much and the marketing people will think it's too little.

Client-side middle managers are pretty candid about money when the boss isn't around. Whether the CEO intends it or not, tech marketers in these sectors are actually charged with baseline sales support, not growing market share. "Marketing budget as a percent of sales? What a concept!" one manager laughed. "Try zero over any number you want."

Here are a few insights from corporate managers about their budgeting process. You'll find the good, the bad, and the ugly here, so adapt anything you find useful and ignore the rest. (These comments were gathered between December 1999 and April 2000.)

"We're a high-growth Internet business in a mature sector where some evangelizing is necessary. Our marketing budget was 150% of sales in year one and 62% of sales in year two. Total outlay for marketing in year two has been about $17 million. This includes product and corporate marketing, field sales support, advertising and PR, and business development. It counts personnel expenses, travel, and overhead. We've gone from zero to $27.4 million in revenues in 24 months."

"Like most engineering-driven companies, the attitude here is 'We know our customers and they know us, so why advertise?' My advertising budget for a $4.5 million product line with a gross margin of 20% is $2,000 a year."

"I'm always dealing with an underfunded marketing effort. I dutifully go through the budgeting tasks and request, say, $200,000—bare bones—to achieve my sales objectives. Through some mysterious process it turns into $40,000 and the sales target is increased."

"Our firm does approximately $50 million in revenues and my marketing budget is .5% of sales! We still spend the largest portion on printed literature and product catalogs. Advertising? It's been so long since we've done any I've forgotten what it is."

"My company's marketing budget is about 3.25 percent of revenues. This figure includes advertising, promotion, travel, sales meetings, and trade shows."

Merrill Chapman's marketing cost matrix

You still want a price list, don't you? You're in luck. The third edition of *The Product Marketing Handbook for Software*, by Merrill R. Chapman, includes the best pricing guide I've seen. It's reproduced here with permission.

Chapman's numbers are realistic as of this writing (3rd quarter 2000). For the next 12 months or so, figure on a plus-or-minus 15% price differential depending upon your geographic location and the type and size of the firm doing the work.

POSITIONING, PRICING AND NAMING	COSTS
Naming Studies	$3K-$50K
Legal Fees	
Basic Trademark Search	$150
Comprehensive National	$1K
Comprehensive International	$2K
Resolve Potential Conflict	$6K
Positioning Studies	
Focus Groups	$K-$10K per session
Market Research	$10K-$300K
Informal Research	$2K-$3K
Pricing Studies	
Focus Groups	$5K-$10K per session
Market Research	$10K-$75K
COLLATERALS	
End-User Collateral	
(Assumes 10M initial print run)	
Brochures (4-color)	$200 per thousand, assume a
	minimum set-up charge of $12 for
	any size run.
Case studies	$1K-$2K for writing
Collateral CDs	$1.50-$3.00 per piece
	(includes production)

Comparison Sheets (2-color)	$150 per thousand
Corporate piece	$250 per thousand
Demo disk	$7.5K-$60K
Design	$750-$3K per piece
Electronic presentations	$1K-$5K per template
Folders	$450 per thousand
NFS SOFTWARE (NOT FOR SALE)	
Full	$10-$35
Partial	$1.5-750
Reprints	$0.25-$1 per page, B&W
Spec Sheets (2-color)	$150 per thousand
SYSTEM OVERVIEW	
Design	$1.5-$3K
Writing	$1.5-$7K
Printing	$150 per thousand
VIDEOS	
Production	$60-$150 per hour
Tapes	$1.50-$2.50 per unit, depending
	on packaging
Talent	$100-$350 per hour
White Paper (Design and writing costs)	$5K-$10K
Channel Collateral	
Corporate Identity Manual	$200-$400
Comparison Sheets (2-color)	$150 per thousand
NFS	
Full	$10-$25
Partial	$1.50-$7.50
Order forms	$75 per thousand
Sell scripts (Design)	$3-$5K per thousand
Spec Sheets (1-color)	$75 per thousand
Merchandising Collateral	
(Assumes runs of 500 units)	

End-caps	$3-$4 per piece
Kiosks	$15-$20 per piece
Mobiles	$.25-$1.50 per piece
Monitor Wraps	$.75-$1.50 per piece
Shelf Talkers (Assumes run of 500)	$.10-$.15 per piece
Tent Cards	$.25-$1.50 per piece
Packaging	
Design	$3K-$5K
Printing (includes box and printing costs)	
Setup Box	$1.50 per box
Tuck Box	$1.10-$1.15 per box
Assembly	
Insert individual piece	$.10-$.25
Shrink Wrap	$0.15
Print Manuals (Assumes one piece with a 2-color cover)	
100+ pages	$1.10-1.50 per unit
200+ pages	$1.75-2.25 per unit
300+ pages	$2.50-3.00 per unit
Duplication (disks)	$.10-$.25 per floppy
Duplication (CDs)	$.50-$.85 per CD
Documentation Creation	
100+ pages	$7.5-$12.5K
200+ pages	$15K-$25K
300+ pages	$30K+
CHANNEL PROMOTIONS	
Distributor	
Ad Placements	$4K-$20K
Basic participation fees	$0-$10K
Buying Incentive	1%-2% of selling price
Catalogs	$1.5K-$2K
Co-op	50% matching funds
Detailing	$40-$60 per store

DM Programs	$2.50-$5.00 per piece
Product Management Services	$5K-10K per year
PR Programs	$1.5-$5K per year
Publications	$1K-$10K per placement
Reseller Presentations	$1.5K-$7K per event
SPIFs	5%-20% of selling price
Technical Training	$0-$2K per hour
Telemarketer Presentations	$750-$2K
Telemarketer Programs	$0-$10K
Trade Show Appearances	$2K-$10K per show
Vendor Nights	$1.5K-$2.5K
Web Site Listings	$500-$10K per listing
Reseller	
Ad Placements	$4K-$20K
Bundling	80%-90% off SRP, may be
	100% off SRP
Buying Incentive	1%-2% of selling price
Catalogs	$750-$10K
Co-op	50% matching funds
Demo Days	$35-$50 per store
Detailing	$40-$60 per store
DM Programs	$2.50-$5.00 per piece
In-store Kiosks	$3K per month
In-store merchandising	$7K-$60K per month
Product Management Services	$5K-$10K per year
PR Programs	$1.5-$5K per year
Publications	$1K-$10K per placement
SPIFs	5%-20% of selling price
Telemarketer Presentations	$750-$2K
Trade Show Appearances	$2K-$10K per show
Web Site Listings	$500-$10K per listing
PR AND PRODUCT REVIEWS	
Review Management	
Review Guide	$5K-$15K
Pre-Release Editorial Tour (Assumes no use of agency, includes travel expenses)	$15K-$20K
Pre-release Editorial Tour Through Agency (10-city tour, does not include travel expenses)	$25K-$35K

PR Rep On Tour With Publisher	$1.2K-$1.5 per day
PR Management	
Launch Event	$5K-$20K
Press Kit	$2K-$3K (Design)
Press Mailings	$1K for 300 pieces
Business Wire Posts	$500
Electronic Posts	$100-$250
ADVERTISING	
Cost of development	$5K-$70K
Placement Fees	15% of ad cost
Cost by Magazine (Assumes 1-page, 4-color ad)	
First Rank (i.e., PC Magazine)	$40K
Second Rank (i.e., PC World)	$15-$35K
Niche (i.e., Publish Magazine)	$1K-$6K
Channel (i.e., CRW)	$1K-$15K
Industry Specific (i.e., The American Law Journal)	$1K-$8K
SALES PROMOTIONS	
Bundling Promotions	
Product Costs	$0-$20
Design Development	$3K-$25K
Fulfillment	$5-$30
Price Promotions	20%-70%, depending on market and product
Free/Premium Offers	
Product	$0-$20
Books	$3-$5
Paraphernalia	$2-$15

DIRECT MARKETING	
Bingo Cards	$.02-$.05 per impression
Direct Fax	$.10-$.30 per minute
Direct Mail	
Per Piece (Standard)	$1.25-$2.50
Per Piece (Multi-dimensional)	$2.00-$6.00
Design (All pieces in mailing)	$10K
Copy (All pieces in mailing)	$4K
Cover letter	$24 per thousand
Brochure	$40 per thousand
Order form	$18 per thousand
Return envelope	$16 per thousand
Cover envelope	$20 per thousand
Postage	$.20-$3.20
Fulfillment (Assumes taking order, processing, and shipping)	$5-$12
Infomercials	$75K-$250K
Telemarketing & Telesales	
Inbound operator costs	$1.50-$2.50 per call
Inbound script and setup	$500 to $750
Outbound operator	$30 to $40 per operator
Outbound script and setup	$1K-$2K
Initial tests	$500 to $1.5K
BUNDLING	
Cost of bundled product	$0-$30
Cost of promotion	$10K-$70K
Cost of packaging (assumes box reengineering)	$1.5-$3
Cost of fulfillment	$1-$5 per piece
Cost of support (assumes extra costs of supporting third-party product, regardless of contractual terms)	$.25-$.80

ELECTRONIC MARKETING	
Kiosk	$1K-$2K
	(usually MDF expenditure)
Web Site Development	
Static Site	$2.5K-$20K
Dynamic Site	$20K-$150K
CD-ROM Distribution	$1K-$12K or an extra
	5%-10% off SRP
Web Ad Development	
Banners	$1.5-$25K, highly dependent on
	scope of project
Web Search Engine Submissions	$30-$100 for software
Web Advertising	
CPM	$.01-$.05 per impression
Click Through	$.30-$.50 per click through
Electronic Direct Marketing	
Bulk mailings	$50-$500 per bulk list
	(Varies widely)
Opt-in	$.15-$.50 per person
TRADESHOWS	
Regional Shows (Northeast Computer Show)	$5K-$25K
Major Shows (i.e. PC Expo)	$15K-$150K
Theme Shows (Networld, OS/2 World)	$15K-$150K
COMDEX	$75K-$500K
Suite	$8K-$25K

Half Your Marketing Budget Goes Down The Drain.

Here's How To Get It Back

The best marketers in the world can't generate big revenues from an itty-bitty budget. The more market share you want, the more you must spend.

This doesn't mean you can't make every dollar work harder. Most marketing programs entail prodigious waste. Here are ways to minimize that waste, leverage your spending, and get somebody else to foot part of the bill.

Make a plan before you commit to anything. How much time did your company spend writing and updating your marketing plan this year? If the answer's "none," you're a target for every open hand that comes along. If the answer's "more than a week or two," you're bogging down in an unproductive process.

To make the connection between money and a marketing plan, think about the requests you get every day. Salespeople clamoring for collateral, media reps with a really, *really* great deal, product managers asking for another $10,000 research report. All urgent requests, all legitimate.

Say yes to everybody and you'll burn through the budget in Q1, then regret it for the rest of the year. Say no to everybody and you'll miss some terrific opportunities. You need a plan that will accommodate last-minute changes but impose enough structure to keep random spending in check.

Workable plans are no more than a few pages long and can be condensed down to a one-page tactical calendar. Anything more complicated is impractical. If you're saddled with a six-pound marketing document complete with SWOT analysis and appendices, put it in the round file or back on the shelf.

On page 158 is an example of the one-page marketing calendar Folio Z uses. Help yourself to it. I like this particular layout because any coverage gaps show up immediately, but there are dozens of ways to represent the same idea.

Start by figuring out your overall marketing budget. Armed with this information, your marketing staff can determine allocations and itemize specific tactics, by audience, on the vertical axis and a timeline (weeks, months, quarters, whatever makes sense) along the horizontal axis.

There's a dot in every square where a tactic intersects with a due date. You can see all your marketing activity, by audience and date, at a glance for the entire year. Scan it for gaps. Is the first quarter overloaded and the back half of the year empty? Rearrange the schedule to keep the communication flow consistent all year. Do certain audiences need extra attention? Beef up the contact type and/or frequency for that group.

Hold the calendar to one page, keep it simple, and keep it in front of everybody who needs to know what's happening. Now your sales force can see that, yes, the marketing people really *do* plan to advertise in *BingBong Monthly* this year, and no, they haven't forgotten to build a Web site revamp into the 3rd-quarter budget.

Client Name

Marketing Communications Calendar
Goal:
Budget:

	Apr	May	Jun	Jul	Aug	Sep	Oct	Nov	Dec	Jan	Feb	Mar
Awareness												
Ads (full page)		•				•				•		
(partial)				•				•			•	•
Lead Generation												
Direct Mail												
Sales Support												
Proposal kit		•										
ROI calculator					•							
Events												
Trade show				•								
Breakfast seminars							•		•			•
Other												
Corporate brochure						•						
Interactive												
Web site revamp									•			
email campaign		•		•			•		•		•	

Folio Z
The Technology Marketing Authority

Pay attention to what doesn't get done.

If more than 25% of the tasks on your calendar never actually materialize, or if you spend more than 25% of the budget on stuff that wasn't on the grid, your marketing problem isn't lack of money—it's lack of focus. This corporate equivalent of Attention Deficit Disorder shows up in three ways:

Chronically delayed or nixed projects. They're a dead giveaway that marketing isn't a priority for your company. Maybe you keep getting distracted by "more important" things, or maybe you weren't serious about the planning process to begin with. Either way, you're tying up money and energy that can be put to better use.

If your initial plans were too ambitious, scale back and focus only on work you're committed to funding and completing. Be honest with yourself and your staff about priorities here, or you'll pay for half-baked projects that do nothing but suck money out of the company.

Seat-of-the-pants decisions. If your marketing people can't stick to the discipline of a one-page calendar, or if you change your mind so often the calendar is useless, you'll sacrifice the leverage that comes with consistency. Entrepreneurs are notoriously inconsistent. If that's your management style, fine—but don't kid yourself. This is a very expensive way to run a business.

160   *Market hubris.* I've said it before and I'll say it again: it's
impossible for a 21st-century technology company to build
market share quickly without market segmentation. No matter how well-funded your firm or how terrific your product,
you do *not* have enough money or time to make inroads using
a horizontal strategy. Target two or three vertical segments
and build from there.

When you can't squeeze your marketing calendar down to
a single page because you've "targeted" so many audiences, or
you funnel money into projects that aren't even on the calendar, your focus problem is diluting every dollar you spend.

Don't play the second-guessing game. Project costs are directly
related to the number of people in the approval process.
Agencies watch their clients flush staggering amounts of
money down the drain at this stage, and there's not much we
can do about it.

Subject-matter experts are invaluable early on, but every
time they pop up at the last minute with one more piece of
data, the revisions cost money. Equally costly are senior managers who remain hands-off until the 11th hour, then slash
and burn when it's their turn to review the work.

Managing these people (including yourself, if you're one of
the culprits) is one of the most effective cost-cutting moves
you can make. To hold the line on spending, give one person—somebody with guts and authority—the final say, and
don't second-guess his or her decision.

Don't strive for perfection. I've seen project costs double or triple while clients vacillated on a decision. I've seen business opportunities evaporate as salespeople squabbled over ad copy. I've watched excellent marketing people pack up and go when their CEO announced yet another strategy change. And I've seen thousands of dollars worth of collateral dumped into trash bags because somebody didn't like the color.

Striving for perfection is wasteful. If you're serious about spending your marketing money wisely, aim for consistency, clarity, and frequency above all, and don't sweat the small stuff.

Make your ads do double duty. When you run a new print advertisement, order reprints. Reprints are available from the magazines that publish your ads, and they're cheap: usually under a dollar apiece when ordered in quantities of a thousand or so, and the more you order the lower the unit cost. The flip side of a reprint is prime selling space, so don't waste it. Fill it with something useful or interesting (preferably both).

Using reprints as follow-on direct mail can actually triple the effectiveness of your ad campaign. They're also useful in sales folders, recruiting packets, and press kits. Use them as handouts at trade shows, and insert them into employees' pay envelopes. (Believe it or not, some people never see their company's ads.)

Buy full rights to design work and use it on multiple pieces. Graphic designers own the art they produce, so unless the contract says otherwise, you're entitled to use the image only once. Buy out the rights (you'll pay an upcharge for this, but you'll amortize it every time you reuse the work) and repeat the image, or elements of it, throughout your entire campaign.

Two years ago we asked a client to spend a big chunk of his creative budget on one 9" x 12" illustration. Today, elements of that illustration have been used in multiple direct-mail campaigns and appear on his advertising, product packaging, Web site, collateral materials—even golf shirts. When he introduces himself and his company, people say, "Oh yeah. You're the guys with the walking fish." *That's* what consistency and frequency will get you.

Tap into co-op marketing programs. Co-op advertising is a way of life for manufacturers and traditional retailers, but technology companies that don't sell through retail channels are unaware of this hidden gold mine. There's a ton of money out there if you know where to look. Of the billions of dollars in co-op marketing programs, one-third goes unused.

What is a co-op program? Loosely defined, it's an expense-sharing mechanism. Let's say your product runs on BigBucks hardware. If BigBucks offers a co-op allowance to authorized business partners and you're willing to include their logo in your ads, BigBucks may pony up funds to cover a percentage of your advertising costs. There are dozens of variations on this theme, but the underlying goal is to piggyback on each others' strengths.

Co-op deals range from traditional advertising programs to a simple arrangement between two companies with similar interests. Vendors who are after the same prospects you are can be good co-op partners. At least one technology company transformed its customer newsletter several years ago into a full-blown magazine funded by non-competing advertisers, and it's one of the most effective marketing tools I've seen.

Market development funds and programs available from distributors and resellers are another resource, but be cautious. These direct marketing programs, technical training, product management services, press releases, or Web site listings can cost two or three times what you'd spend in-house.

How do you find out about co-op opportunities? Start by asking your ad agency. If you don't have an agency (and even if you do), assess all your business relationships. Who has a vested interest in reaching the same targets you do? Conversely, who's got resources or access that are important to you?

Don't overlook your own service providers. Printers, bankers, payroll services, management consultants, even your ad agency may jump all over an opportunity to cosponsor one of your marketing projects in exchange for attribution. Think creatively. You'll find money in unexpected places when you look hard enough.

8

TALENT: FIND THE BEST, LOSE THE REST

- *Why you don't need a marketing manager…yet*

- *Hand-off or standoff? The marketing/sales relationship*

- *What every good marketer should know*

WHY YOU DON'T NEED A MARKETING MANAGER ... YET

The day will come, early in your in com-
pany's life, when you'll decide to hire a mar-
keting manager. The idea usually kicks in
after a couple of successful quarters.
Projections look good, sales activity is hum-
ming along, leads are popping up, and your
company's beginning to get attention from
the marketplace and the press. You've been
spearheading the marketing initiative so far,

but you want to focus on other areas. Delegating sounds like a great idea.

Maybe it is. Just make sure you're delegating, not dumping. And be sure you're realistic about what the person you're hiring can, and will, do. Many emerging tech firms falter unnecessarily when the CEO steps away from the marketing function, especially when the intermediary is well-meaning but inexperienced.

If your head count is below about 30 and your revenues are still below the $5 million mark, it's probably too soon to leave marketing in somebody else's hands. These are broad guidelines, obviously, but until you pass certain benchmarks the responsibility should stay with you.

Why? Because *nobody* burns money faster than a marketing newbie—and newbies are about all a small firm with a small budget can afford. "Newbie" in this context means two things: young and inexperienced or seasoned but inexperienced in your business. Either way, you'll pay dearly for on-the-job training, often in ways you won't discover until it's too late. (You'll also be distancing yourself from a crucial aspect of the business at exactly the wrong time.)

Here's a true story. Several years ago my agency was retained by a software firm with a good product and a generous budget (an attractive combination). The marketing manager was an MBA who had been hired away from the advertising department at Kentucky Fried Chicken.

She was smart and experienced, but this was her first foray

into business-to-business software. During the first 30 days she hired an assistant, drew up a detailed marketing plan, and directed us to create all-new sales collateral and a national ad campaign.

Within six months the assistant was gone, the new corporate brochure was in its 27th (yes, 27th) revision, and the ad campaign was running in half a dozen overlapping trade magazines. (She bought the media herself and the reps offered "discounts" too good to pass up.) At the end of the first year she'd blown through half a million dollars and the collateral still wasn't off the press. The sales force was bitching about no leads and the controller was pressing her hard about budget overruns.

"Where was the agency while all this was going on?" you ask. Well, we were back at the ranch making endless copy and layout revisions. Although the marketing director didn't yet fully understand her company's product or sales process, she wanted to be our sole contact. The briefing info she provided was sketchy (and in some cases wrong), so every draft we wrote needed major rewrites after the product people and salespeople saw them. This happened not just once, but over and over.

When an agency screws up because it can't, or won't, learn your business, that's one thing. But if it's given bad information from the get-go—and no access to sources who can correct it—you'll pay dearly for rework. This company's brochure alone cost $64,000 more than the original estimate because of a well-meaning but inexperienced marketing manager.

It's a dilemma. If you can't afford an industry veteran but you're drowning in detail, what are you supposed to do?

Get tactical help. Find good freelancers or a small agency to handle your creative needs (copy, design, collateral) on a project basis. And hire a marketing coordinator to handle the project logistics. Don't relinquish key decisions like budget approvals, strategic planning, and creative sign-off until you can afford a marketing manager who has truly earned the title.

Finally, if you have someone on staff with good marketing potential, don't be stingy with professional training. Good talent is hard to find, especially in the IT sector. Growing your own is a great way to get it. Sure, it takes time and patience…but there's no free lunch anywhere.

What to look for in a marketing manager

- *Experience.* Look for a minimum of seven to 10 years of experience in the marketing field…somebody who has been there and done it before, many times over.

- *Passion.* Look for someone who is genuinely excited by marketing and what it can achieve…passionate marketing directors tend to have better ideas, more creative concepts, and a more compelling way of addressing the problem or the opportunity.

- *Street smarts.* Marketing is not always the science that business people would like to believe it is. In few other fields do insight, intuition, and gut response have a greater bearing upon development of strategy and decision-making. Look for a candidate who has an intuitive understanding of the marketplace and the consumer and can convert that understanding into direction and action.

• *Decisive manner.* Because most marketing environments are known for their lack of perfect information, the field can be a disaster area for indecisive managers. A lot of marketing failure occurs because decisions are second-guessed and delayed until it's too late.

Good marketing directors will sometimes make bad decisions, but that's part of the process. The more important determinant is hiring somebody who has the experience and confidence to make a decision and take a stand.

—Alf Nucifora

H AND - OFF OR STANDOFF? THE MARKETING/SALES RELATIONSHIP

There's an uneasy truce between sales and marketing in the best of times. This becomes a dysfunctional turf battle when the company's under pressure. Trigger events—senior management changes, a new competitor on the scene, a lost deal, or a shaky account—create anxiety that affects performance. And when sales performance suffers, everybody suffers.

The signs are subtle at first. On the sales

side, "B" players start to miss their quotas. Deals that were a sure thing don't close. The pipeline shrinks a little; the sales cycle expands a little, and it takes more leads to generate a qualified prospect.

In the marketing department, inquiries are slowing down and there seem to be more tire-kickers in the mix. It's taking longer to produce ads and collateral, and the marketing people shrug off direct questions from the sales force.

Now the finger-pointing begins. The VP of sales says the ad campaign stinks; the marketing VP says the campaign works just fine, but the salespeople just won't follow up the leads.

After awhile you'll lose patience. You'll tell the marketing VP to fire the agency and bring in a new one, and you'll tell the sales VP to hire a consultant. If it goes on too long, you'll let both of them go—and the spiral takes another downward turn.

Salespeople and marketing people don't really understand each other. Salespeople think all it takes to be successful in marketing is luck and a big budget. Marketers think selling is just a matter of persistence and "people skills." As important as they are to each other, neither knows how the other makes a living.

Sales competence is judged by how much you sell. Marketing competence is judged by how much you know. Salespeople are measured with excruciating precision, while marketing people often aren't measured at all. This in itself is a recipe for resentment—and it's a big problem for you, the CEO.

It *is* possible to create an effective working relationship between sales and marketing, starting with fundamental expectations for both sides. These expectations must come from the top or they won't have any teeth.

Expect your marketing people to:
- Understand clearly how your company makes and loses money
- Ask customers and prospects face-to-face what they think of your marketing materials
- Base a portion of their compensation on performance
- Consistently turn up new firsthand information about your prospects and buyers

Expect your salespeople to:
- Make joint sales calls with people from the marketing department
- Do it again, this time visiting someone who has recently seen or received your latest marketing material
- Do it again, this time with a difficult prospect
- Do it again, and make this one a cold call

For salespeople, the moment of truth is face-to-face with the buyer. For marketers, there's often no connection between revenues and what they do every day.

Once they close that gap, stand back.

WHAT EVERY GOOD MARKETER SHOULD KNOW

When your marketing department has a credibility problem, the whole company pays for it. Senior management intervention is the only way to solve it, because delegating down the chain does nothing but generate a lot of tap dancing and finger pointing.

When marketing people consistently fail to deliver, the problem usually boils down to one (or more) of the following:

- *They're confused about your product, market, or business.*

- They get mixed signals about their role in the organization.
- They don't know how they're being measured.
- They accepted their position—but they didn't pursue it.

In the worst case, your marketing department consists of nothing but people like these. (It happens all the time. If your organization is very large or very small, the more likely that is. I once worked for a $4 billion company with a marketing staff of 42, none professionally trained for their jobs. How often would that happen in accounting, manufacturing, or R&D?)

Marketing people are about as far away from the cash register as you can get.

—William Kennedy, PK Data

You can fix all these problems but the last one. There's a whole tribe of people out there who graduated with liberal-arts degrees, moved into the work force, gravitated to communications-type positions, and just kept getting promoted. Another scenario: the salesperson-named-marketing-manager scenario, where everybody thinks the skills are interchangeable and can't figure out why they aren't.

These people tend to self-select when they've been at their careers for about seven years. At that point they settle in as middle managers in a low-pressure environment or leave the field altogether.

Going back to the trouble spots mentioned above, here's what you can—and must—do to clear them up. The list below describes minimum expectations for each member of your marketing staff. Expect new hires to complete this to-do list during their first four months on the job. For existing staff, schedule things in a group or individually, but get them out of the office and into the field immediately. If you hire people without this experience, give it to them. If you can't or won't give it to them, accept the fact that your marketing department is actually a production and distribution center for sales literature, and don't expect much more.

A qualified marketing person has:

- Accompanied a salesperson on at least three prospect calls
- Used your product(s) or seen live demos of each
- Personally interviewed (in person or on the phone) a dozen customers for customer satisfaction surveys or case studies
- Interviewed two or more salespeople to learn about the sales cycle, their ideal and actual prospects, and how marketing can help them sell
- Interviewed one or more prospects who decided not to buy

180

- A clear understanding about how your company makes money, where your company loses money, and which aspects of your business are most and least profitable

- Read your competition's literature and advertising and know what they're claiming, where they're winning, and how your company sells against them

- Identified three publications relevant to buyers and influencers in your market and reads them regularly

---

I am a marketing consultant and, yes, I have resigned accounts before. As a consultant (I don't care how good you are) you live hand-to-mouth. Nothing is guaranteed, which makes turning business away difficult. At the same time, you want to work with companies who understand, appreciate, and value well-planned marketing. Unfortunately, this is not always the case. In fact, I have found that the majority of marketing directors haven't the slightest inkling what marketing is. As Roger Peterson and Nicholas De Bonis explain in Managing Business-to-Business Marketing Communications, *all too often somebody (usually the seniormost sales guy) walks into the office on Monday morning to learn that he is now the "marketing director," a job for which he has little inclination and even less aptitude to handle.*

In the industrial sector, this situation is often exacerbated by the fact that the corporate culture stresses product design and engineering ("Look at this cool product we designed! I wonder who would want to buy it.") And marketing is often a euphemism for "trying to get folks to agree that this widget is really neat."

As a consultant, I try my best to work within this system. Occasionally, however, the marketing director and I don't see eye-to-eye. In those cases, I have no problem walking away from what I believe to be a losing proposition.

I am also an industrial copywriter (in fact, that is how I make the majority of my income). Occasionally, I work with companies through an ad agency. This is, by far, the most frustrating situation of all. Many times, the agency principals are not marketing people and do not either appreciate or pay attention to the marketing basics that govern their client's industry. They are interested in the creative aspect. Although my background is with ad agencies, I have no patience for this kind of masquerade (fraud, really). When I attempt to do the marketing legwork that they should be doing, I am usually shielded from the client. As a result, the information and guidance that the client could use are being intercepted by the very agency that should be supplying it. When this happens, I resign the business in good conscience.

—*Alan Silverman*
Writing with the Voice of Reason

Set measurable goals or settle for mush

Once your marketing people have the necessary field experience, check out their job descriptions—if they exist. Does everybody in your marketing department have a written job description that includes measurable performance requirements? I'll bet they don't.

If I'm wrong, great. If not, decide right now what you want to see in terms of measurable results. It doesn't make sense to complain about vague paybacks from your marketing investment if you don't tell people exactly what you expect.

Measuring performance is a fact of life on the operating side of the business. Marketing doesn't have to be any different. What do you care about? Lead generation? Conversion to sales? Increases in awareness? Customer retention? The number of projects produced? Spell it out, attach a number to it, and don't make it too overwhelming. Three key benchmarks are plenty. Just make sure they're clear.

Mixed messages about marketing in the rest of the organization

You know, now I can laugh about my old bosses referring to marketing as "the black hole of profits," but I wasn't laughing at the time. It hurt. Doing a job that management considers a profit drain rather than a contribution doesn't do much for morale.

Times are different now: most CEOs are well aware of how important marketing is to the company's success. So if you're not convinced your marketing department is earning its keep, it is your responsibility to define the rules and then hire, grow, and compensate people who can play by them and win.

House rules for senior management

- Expect your marketing department to think strategically.

- Keep your paws off the day-to-day.

- Require a written marketing plan every year.

- Compensate marketing people for performance.

- Require sales and marketing to communicate regularly.

- Don't make decisions by committee, and don't expect your staff to.

House rules for marketers

- If management hovers, ask point-blank what it will take to earn some breathing room.

- If you're not asked to produce a written marketing plan, do it anyway and present it in person.

- Know your company's revenues, expenses, chief competitors, primary sources of income, business threats, and operating budgets.

- Understand exactly what it takes to make and deliver your product or service.

- Learn things about your prospects/customers that nobody else in the company knows.

- YOU measure inquiries, leads, conversions,

trade- show attendees, phone calls, letters of praise.

- Keep sales and management informed about what your department's doing, especially your successes and discoveries.

- Spend your company's money as if it were your own.

9

RESULTS: IS THIS
STUFF WORKING?

- *What to measure and what to ignore*

- *The useful copycat*

- *What do you say to the ones who get away?*

- *What you can learn from your company's tombstone*

WHAT TO MEASURE AND WHAT TO IGNORE

Last week I asked a client what return he was expecting from a trade-show mailing. His expectations were too high, so I had to educate him. "If it costs $300 for a personal sales call and $900 to close a sale, why do you expect a postcard to yield the same results for 78 cents?" He didn't laugh.

—Online marketing forum participant

Most CEOs fall into one of four camps when it comes to measuring results. The first group is clueless but blasé: "My company doesn't worry about results. We're building a brand."

The second group is clueless and irritable: "There's got to be a way to measure this stuff, and if my agency people were any good they'd be doing it."

The third group is obsessed. These CEOs want every activity, no matter how inconsequential, sliced, diced, and cross-tabbed. They ask for big, fat reports that nobody reads.

The fourth group is pragmatic. These CEOs expect their marketing people to do whatever is necessary to get useful information, but no more. This group makes more progress than the first three combined, because these CEOs don't overcomplicate the measurement issue.

Here's a true story—embarrassing, but instructive.

Years ago I worked with a mainframe software company that sold back-office administration systems to insurance companies. During my tenure the firm was approached by a buyer, due diligence got under way, and the acquiring management team made a site visit.

When these people showed up in the marketing department we felt like third-graders in the principal's office. The head guy was enamored with sales force automation (a new concept at the time), and convinced that no marketing department could be effective without one. He looked right at me and said, "How does this company determine lead-to-sale ratios? What's the conversion rate? Where did the last deal come from?"

I was speechless. "I don't know," I admitted.

As soon as he left I came to my senses. Tracking system, schmacking system. The salesperson who did the deal knew darn well where the lead came from, and so did the marketing department. Any company that closes only four sales in two years needs common sense, not automated analysis. This situation taught me an important lesson. If you want a practical answer, don't overcomplicate the question.

Four rules for measuring marketing results

1. Measure one thing at a time.

2. Measure it long enough to know what's really happening.

3. Make incremental, not massive, changes.

4. Do more of what works and less of what doesn't.

How do you decide what's working and what isn't? There are probably as many answers as there are business-school professors, but most of them are hogwash. Formulas and statistics aren't helpful in day-to-day operations. Just pay attention to three indicators: the length of your sales cycle, your cost per sale, and the tactics in your marketing mix that yield the best return.

Track all three for 12 months to establish benchmarks. In year two you'll notice trends, and in year three you'll have enough data to see where the potholes and the opportunities lie. Now do more of what works and less of what doesn't.

Include a call to action (CTA) on your marketing material. Offers—discounts, refunds, useful information, promotional items, opportunities to win, anything tangible—are the most effective CTAs, since most people won't act unless they get something tangible in return. The weakest CTA is the one you see most often: "Call now for more information." Note: 80% of B2B buyers go directly to the Web to research purchases. Make your offer contingent upon a visit to your Web site.

Assign responsibility for tracking and logging lead information. "If it's everybody's job, it's nobody's job," I once heard a successful entrepreneur say, and he's right. (Especially when the job is one nobody really wants in the first place.) If you're serious about measuring your marketing performance, tracking leads accurately—from first contact to final disposition—is imperative. The person in charge must bird-dog the salespeople, keep good records, and know what marketing activities are taking place when.

Find out for yourself where the leads go. One-hundred percent of inquiries should be followed up. Ha! Everybody knows what happens to trade-show leads: they're dumped into a

shoebox and warehoused on the marketing manager's credenza. Who knows what gems lie among the tire-kickers in
that box? The best way to find out what happens to leads in
your company is to trace their path a few times yourself.

Use bridge pages to identify your Web site visitors. Let's say you
run an ad offering a t-shirt to the first 500 visitors who solve
a puzzle on your Web site. Use a bridge page to intercept and
identify those respondents before giving them access to the
quiz. (Be prepared for some visitors to drop out at this stage
and others to give you bogus information.) If you prefer, use
the bridge page simply to count traffic. By publishing the
bridge page URL only in selected media, the hit rate will tell
you how effectively those media are generating response.

*Make sure your salespeople ask prospects how they heard about
your company.* This is the world's most common-sense tracking technique, but it's amazing how few companies do it.
When inside and outside salespeople—and anybody who
answers incoming calls or email from prospects—make a
habit of asking, "How did you hear about us?" you'll gather
useful data. Tape a message to the telephone reminding people to ask the question, and give everybody a list of the current ad schedule.

Establish benchmarks. It's impossible to measure anything
without a point of reference. Executives who complain about
the lack of accountability in advertising but won't fund surveys to find out where they stand right now, today, have noth-

ing to complain about. Nobody's going to measure your progress until you make it a priority. That means you'll need to spend time and money on it.

Since you're aiming for multiple outcomes with your marketing, benchmark each of these areas:

Awareness—How many people in your target market know your company exists? Of that group, how many know what your company does?

Trust—Where do you rank in relation to your competitors as a trusted source? How many of your current customers would refer you positively to a friend or colleague?

Value—How does your product measure up to the other options your buyers have?

Margins—Is your goal to attract more profitable customers? Benchmark the average margin per customer (or per sale).

Retention—Is your goal to keep and cross-sell customers? Benchmark accordingly.

Sales volume and market share—These are obvious. How much of the market do you have on day one? How much do you have at the end of the measurement period? Measure sales volume the same way.

Don't approve marketing initiatives that don't include an evaluation component. This is a common-sense recommendation, but trickier to execute than it first seems. Who's responsible for the evaluation? Some CEOs assume this is the agency's role; others expect their marketing staff to handle it. Make your expectations clear and put them in writing. (You don't need an elaborate memo, just a note saying "here's what I want to know 90 days after the campaign is launched.")

If this is the agency's responsibility, provide access to inside information. You must also agree on compensation if the firm hasn't included post-project evaluation in its estimates.

Feedback from the field

For general direct mail campaigns we purchase names from trade publications for 10 cents to 30 cents each. When we buy from Dun & Bradstreet the names cost from $1.50 to over $10 each. In either case, we can expect to close about 2% of these leads in a mail campaign with telesales follow-up.

Our company quantifies the value of trade shows by dividing the cost of the show by the number of leads we generate. Leads can cost anywhere from $25 to over $1,000 each, but typically they run about $110 each. When our booth personnel qualify the leads, we expect over 80 percent will be true prospects and we'll close on about 25% of them.

THE USEFUL COPYCAT

Never imitate your competitors. They don't know what they're doing, either. But pay very close attention when your competitors start imitating you.

In the early days of electronic data interchange (EDI), one of the industry pioneers hired Folio Z to position the company and develop its marketing materials. The charge was to create a solid, blue-chip persona: this 20-person firm needed to sell into Fortune 500 accounts. The materials we produced emphasized safety, security, and solidity.

Three years later the company came back for an overhaul. The competitive landscape was heating up, and our client had evolved from upstart to segment leader. The marketing problem had changed, too: now the task was to switch the positioning from "big company" (synonymous with "unresponsive" and "technical laggard")—while preserving its reputation as an industry leader and innovator.

> "When people are free to do as they please, they usually imitate each other."
>
> —*Anonymous*
>
> "In advertising, not to be different is virtually suicidal."
>
> —*William Bernbach*
>
> "If you ever have the good fortune to create a great advertising campaign, you will soon see someone steal it. This is irritating, but don't let it worry you. Nobody has ever built a brand by imitating someone else."
>
> —*David Ogilvy*

The repositioning look-and-feel we recommended was initially turned down flat. The new concept was based on a stylized character we nicknamed Bart, rendered in brilliant color on a background of solid black. The CEO wasn't comfortable with the dramatic change but he did approve the campaign.

Bart turned up everywhere: on packaging and literature, eight feet tall at trade shows, on t-shirts and baseball caps. The ads generated good readership and recall scores, and the sales force loved Bart because prospects remembered the company he represented.

Eighteen months later a competitor's new ad campaign borrowed heavily from the Bart theme, and our client was delighted. When the competition copies your marketing, you know it's making an impact.

The copycat syndrome goes beyond visual expression. As you become more successful, competitors will preempt your own marketing messages, positions, and claims and use them against you. This is why branding is so important. Companies become associated with certain attributes in the customer's mind *over time*. Pull back too soon and you only make it easier for competitors to poach on your territory.

(Remember the rule of 50? The first 50 times you say something, nobody hears it. The second 50 times, nobody understands it. The third 50 times, nobody believes it. It's the 151st repetition that counts.)

What can you learn from a copycat?

You'll find out who thinks they're competing against you—and who wants to. This is an invaluable early-warning sign. Often you won't recognize these companies any other way. They operate below your radar until they're ready to strike. Watch carefully to see who's patterning their messages after yours.

You'll find out what doesn't work. A copycat gives the priceless gift of objectivity: suddenly you can see your company through someone else's eyes. Are those claims credible? Are those promises worthwhile? Are those credentials valid?

You'll find out what the market thinks you really are. This is a good reality check. If the companies imitating yours aren't firms you want to be compared with, you need to test the market's perceptions against your own. Be forewarned that the market is always right.

WHAT DO YOU SAY
TO THE ONES WHO
GET AWAY?

Until I became a business owner myself, I didn't realize how much courage it takes to ask people why they turned you down. Companies that follow up diligently with lost prospects and employees are rare, and the most painless way to do this is to build ongoing surveys into your marketing mix.

Surveying is an art and a science, and it can be as simple or as complex as you want to make it. Your goal is to gather timely infor-

mation about your customers and prospects. To be useful, that information needs to be predictable and unbiased—or at least as close as you can get.

Statisticians and market researchers will tsk tsk all over the following recommendations, and rightly so. They're not statistically reliable and they're not truly objective. But you know what? They're better than nothing.

By constantly keeping your ear to the ground, you'll pick up rumblings you can work with. The sounds won't be perfectly distinct, but they'll be clear enough to guide and improve your marketing communications.

Three questions to answer before you ask anybody anything:

- What do you want to find out?
- Once you find out, what can you do about it?
- Realistically, what *will* you do about it?

It's easy to waste time crafting surveys that don't address your real priorities but generate reams of useless information. If 80 customers out of 100 say they'd like you to open a branch in Sheboygan but you have no intention of doing so, don't ask the question in the first place.

Marketing expert Dennis Caruso uses a 15-point checklist to keep surveys manageable and effective. This approach makes sense for virtually any audience, including employees, customers, prospects, and lost prospects.

1. Collect, assemble, and analyze the benchmark data.

2. Select your target population.

3. Design the questionnaire. Choose questions that will reveal the truth, not what you "want" to hear or read.

4. Begin by telling respondents that you value their opinion.

5. Explain exactly why you need their help.

6. Make the early questions very easy to answer.

7. Organize the survey in question sets (multiple questions around the same issue) to make it easier for the respondent to stay focused.

8. As much as possible, design questions that can be answered with weighted, multiple-choice responses.

9. Provide at least five possible answers per multiple-choice question.

10. Frame sensitive questions in the least-threatening manner.

11. Ask sensitive questions at least twice. "When you think of widgets, who comes to mind?" "If I were in the market for widgets, who would you recommend?" "Whose widgets do you buy?" This technique helps you validate answers about issues most important to you.

12. Use telesurveys if your budget permits.

13. If executing internally, have your customer

service or inside sales team make the calls. If you outsource, have each of the telesurvey-ors assigned to your project call you before they make any live calls.

14. Test your instrument. Select a small sample (no more than 10); collect and analyze the results. Modify as necessary to proceed on a larger scale.

15. Have more than one person interpret and report upon the collected data, then com-pare notes.

Beyond traditional pen-and-paper, there are a variety of ways to administer surveys. Your Web site is a natural place to ask questions and invite responses. Trade shows are another good venue, and a tool called Zoomerang (www.zoomerang.com) lets marketers take online surveys to a whole new level.

Whose opinion counts? Anybody and everybody who comes into contact with your company. Among them:

Job candidates who turn you down. Many companies conduct exit interviews when an employee leaves, but not many inter-view the candidates who turn down a job offer. In today's labor market, it's up to us to sell ourselves to potential employees rather than vice versa. Those who turn down our offer weren't sold, and you need to know why not.

The best way to find out is to ask. Decide for yourself what instrument makes most sense: follow-up phone call, email, ink-on-paper survey returned to you anonymously. The

results might surprise you, and you'll get a firsthand look at
how you come across to some of the most important people in
your company's life: potential employees.

Candidates that you *turn down.* People who have a good interview experience with your company tell other people about it,
and that goodwill isn't contingent on their receiving a job
offer. Some of our best employees were referred to us by appli-
cants we did not hire.

The positive impression you can make by following up an in-
person interview with a brief "how did we come across?" questionnaire can't be overemphasized. Stay away from issues like
pay comparisons and benefits and ask about the applicant's
impressions of your company. How well does your cultural personality (your brand) come across in an interview situation?

Lost prospects. Catch these people as soon after the sale's been
lost as possible—in fact, within 24 hours if you can. Often
they'll feel guilty about choosing someone else and will be
candid with you to "make up" for it. But the longer you wait,
the less willing they'll be to have the conversation at all.

If you craft your questions carefully, you'll uncover the
buyer's real objections. Product? Price? References? Features?
Chemistry with the salesperson? This information tells you
precisely where to focus your improvements. If you've been
blaming all those lost deals on a salesperson but discover the
real problem is an impossible-to-navigate phone system, don't
jettison the salesperson. Fix the phones.

Former customers. This is often the most difficult group to survey. None of us likes to ask point-blank where we screwed up—especially if we're not likely to get a sugar-coated answer. To make sure it gets done, and to make sure you get candid answers, hire a third-party firm to make these calls.

When you survey this group, you have a responsibility to let your company know the outcome. You are *guaranteed* to meet resistance. In some cases employees will deny the problem; in others they'll lay it squarely in the customer's lap. This is one of the most difficult aspects of asking for feedback: you must do something about it.

Departing employees. If you conduct employee exit interviews, you're probably asking questions about pay and working conditions. That's great—and it's only half the story. Departing employees, more than anyone else, can tell you firsthand how well the firm personifies the brand.

Disgruntled people who aren't leaving by choice won't say anything positive, so their responses are biased. At the other end of the spectrum are those who repeat nothing but platitudes. If you chop off the extremes and pay attention to what's going on in the middle, you'll see how your people epitomize your brand. They will show you, better than anyone, the gap between who you are and who you want to be.

Customer Satisfaction Survey Instructions

Reproduced courtesy of CCH Incorporated.
Downloadable version available at toolkit.cch.com/tools/csrsur

Customer satisfaction is the key to success. You want customers to be happy with the products and services you provide. If they feel they have received good value for their money, your business will prosper. Getting your customers to tell you what's good about your business, and where you need improvement, helps you to be sure that your business measures up to their expectations.

A customer satisfaction survey is one way to gather this vital information. There are any number of ways to get copies to your customers. Copies can be included with orders, mailed directly at regular intervals, sent and received by fax—whatever is convenient for your particular business. Many won't be returned, but those that are will make it worth your while.

The customer satisfaction survey that follows is designed to get your customers to tell you what they really think. No ranking of quality on a scale of one to five, no lengthy questions, just a list of key business activities and space to respond. Limiting the choices to "outstanding" and "needs improvement" sends a clear message that you expect the products and services you supply to be the best available, period. Keeping the survey to a single page makes it more likely that customers will take the time to respond. It also facilitates faxing. Be sure to include instructions on how to return the completed surveys. Give your fax number, include stamped, addressed envelopes, or whatever it takes to make it more likely that you'll get them back.

Don't forget to follow up on the comments you receive. If you have to change a procedure, tell an employee how you want things done, pick a new delivery service, do it. And advertise the fact that you did. Send thank-you notes to the customers whose comments caused you to make a change. Let them know that you can do an even better job because they took the time to help you improve.

Sample Customer Satisfaction Survey

[print on company letterhead]

We are constantly looking for ways to improve the quality of our products and services. To do that, we need to know what you think. We'd really appreciate it if you would take just a few minutes to respond to the handful of questions below. As a valued customer, how you rate our work is the most important information we can get. Please help us do the job you deserve—the best possible!

Please return this survey
[describe how you want the survey returned.]

Please circle "Outstanding" or "Needs Improvement" and comment:

Products: Outstanding   Needs Improvement
_____

Service
and Support: Outstanding   Needs Improvement
_____

Delivery: Outstanding   Needs Improvement
_____

Ordering
and Billing: Outstanding   Needs Improvement
_____

Employees: Outstanding   Needs Improvement
_____

WHAT YOU CAN LEARN FROM YOUR COMPANY'S TOMBSTONE

Picture this. You've burned through your last round of funding, you've outrun your line of credit, the market seemed to shift overnight, and the hotshots you hired in sales and development finally bailed out for better opportunities. You're out of business.

What went wrong?

Usually, it's something obvious to everybody but the people in charge. Most executives know what their weak points are.

What they don't know—consciously, anyway—is which ones might be fatal.

I've seen more than my share of businesses fall apart over the years, and they've all had one thing in common: the management team had one or two collective weaknesses that nobody talked about (not in public, anyway). Eventually these problem areas became their downfall, even though other aspects of the business seemed to be pretty healthy. At Folio Z we call this the Pretend-It's-Not-There syndrome.

I learned long ago that when you're hired to give marketing counsel, it's best to tread cautiously in the personal-advice department. What to do? Pretend-It's-Not-There undermines any marketing initiative, no matter how brilliant, so we had to find a way to talk to clients about it.

"… of all sad words of tongue or pen, the saddest are these: 'It might have been!'"

—John Greenleaf Whittier

One day the answer presented itself in a messaging workshop. One of our account people mentioned The Syndrome in passing and sparked a terrific discussion. That's when we realized that in the context of the workshop (and probably in any other neutral, facilitated setting) people *will* talk honestly about their company's vulnerabilities. That, of course, is a giant step toward overcoming them.

Ask yourself and your executives the same questions we urge our clients to wrestle with. Do it now, while your company's healthy. You'll find them not only a barometer of your management health, but good preventive medicine.

If you're wondering what any of this has to do with marketing, look at the questions again. Your agency and/or your marketing staff should be asking you the same ones—paraphrased, perhaps—before you spend a cent. If you don't know the answers, this is the time to figure them out.

Six questions for your management team

1. If any company were to put us out of business, who would it be?

2. How would they do it?

3. If our company failed tomorrow and we could overhear our competitors gossiping about it, what would they say?

4. What would our worst employee say about our company if he/she thought we'd never hear it?

5. What would our best employee say?

6. If outside investors took over this business tomorrow, what would they change first?

Is your company's epitaph on this list?

Everybody makes marketing mistakes. It's when they happen over and over that they're fatal—no matter how well capitalized you are. The most common causes of death:

- We quit too soon.
- We thought we should wait until we had more money.
- We couldn't decide.
- We lost our courage.
- We wanted to get everybody's approval.
- We didn't think it was right yet.
- We worried about what people might think.
- We weren't having any fun.

10

RESOURCES

BOOKS

The Aegis Product Positioning Workbook. Aegis Resources, Inc., 1999. www.aegis-resources.com 1-877-BUY-PMHB

Chapman, Merrill R. *The Product Marketing Handbook for Software, Third Edition.* Aegis Resources, Inc., 1999. www.aegis-resources.com 1-877-BUY-PMHB

Moore, Geoffrey A. *Crossing the Chasm: Marketing and Selling High-Tech Products to Mainstream Consumers.* HarperBusiness, a division of HarperCollins Publishers, 1995.

Moore, Roberta. *Software Success—How to Craft an Effective Software Marketing Budget.* Qualitative Marketing, 2000. www.qmarketing.com 408-295-5524

Pettis, Chuck. *TechnoBrands: How to create & use "brand identity" to market, advertise and sell technology products.* Chuck Pettis American Management Association, 1995.

Reis, Al. *Focus: The Future of Your Company Depends On It.* HarperBusiness, a division of HarperCollins Publishers, 1996. www.harpercollins.com

MAGAZINES

MC: Technology Marketing Intelligence. www.marketingcomputers.com

NEWSLETTERS

Software Success Weekly Newsletter
www.softwaresuccess.com

The Naming Newsletter, Rivkin & Associates, Inc.
www.namingnewsletter.com

RESEARCH AND SURVEYS

Cahners Business Information, Reed Elsevier PLC
www.cahners.com

The following surveys are published annually by Software Success:
- Software Company Operating Ratio Survey
- Software Industry R & D and Services Survey
- Software Sales and Marketing Survey
- Software Industry M&A, Finance & Valuation Survey
- Software Company Pricing & Licensing Survey
- Software Company Compensation & Staffing Survey

For information contact:
Software Success
11300 Rockville Pike, Suite 1100
Rockville, MD 20852-3030
Phone: (877) 266-7075 or (301) 287-2677
Fax: (301) 816-0037
www.softwaresuccess.com

WEB SITES

CCH Incorporated. "Business Owner's Toolkit."
    www.toolkit.cch.com.

Chevron, Jacques.
    www.jrcanda.com. JRC & A branding specialists.

Deep Canyon Market Intelligence.
    www.deepcanyon.com

Bradmore, Don. "The Marketing Dictionary." Monash University
    www.buseco.monash.edu

Market Tools, Inc. "Zoomerang Online survey tools."
    www.zoomerang.com